AN ALABAMA SCRAPBOOK

Retail Price: $18.00

Published by

Honeysuckle Imprint

511 Pratt Avenue
Huntsville, Alabama 35801

Library of Congress Catalog Card Number: **88-083561**
ISBN: **0-9621455-0-5**

PRINTED IN THE UNITED STATES OF AMERICA

First Printing, October 1988
Second Printing, February 1989

AN
ALABAMA
SCRAPBOOK

ک ک ک

32 Alabamians Remember Growing Up

Compiled and Edited by

Ellen Sullivan

and

Marie Stokes Jemison

ACKNOWLEDGEMENTS

Reverend Solomon S. Seay's memoir published with permission of the Southern Regional Council, Atlanta, Georgia.

Virginia Foster Durr's memoir excerpted from *Up Against Friends and Family*, and published with permission of Marie Stokes Jemison.

Randall Williams' memoir copyright ©1975/76 by The New York Times Company. Reprinted by permission.

Wayne Greenhaw's memoir copyright ©1975/76 by The New York Times Company. Reprinted by permission.

Dr. Richard Arrington, Jr.'s memoir printed with permission of The University of Alabama in Birmingham and the University College History Department, with special thanks to Dr. Virginia Hamilton.

Essie Stallworth McGowin's reminiscences used with permission of the McGowin family.

Excerpts from Ella Lovelace's diary published with permission of Lovelace O. Howard.

Mark Childress's memoir appeared in slightly altered form in *Southern Living*.

Cover photos courtesy of Bettye K. Wray, Dr. Richard Arrington, Jr., Ralph Hammond, Hubert Grissom, and Margaret Jemison.

Cover design by Robin McDonald.

TABLE OF CONTENTS

Introduction ix

Nell Brasher, Sprott 1

John Forney, Tuscaloosa 9

Ella Lovelace, Marion 15

Jesse Hill Ford, Jasper 19

Reverend Solomon S. Seay, Sr., Shorter 23

Virginia Foster Durr, Union Springs 25

Richard Arrington, Jr., Livingston 31

Alvis Howard, Huntsville 39

Ellen Sullivan, Shannon 49

Randall Williams, LaFayette 55

Ned McDavid, Birmingham 59

Janie L. Shores, Georgiana 63

Bettye K. Wray, Birmingham 67

Wayne Greenhaw, Colbert County 73

Helen Shores Lee, Birmingham 77

Jane L. Weeks, Birmingham 83

Michael David Shrader, Tuscumbia 91

Essie Stallworth McGowin, Pineville 95

Gould Beech, Montgomery 99

Hubert Grissom, Jr., Cullman 105

Smith W. Moseley, Selma 111

Jim Reed, Tuscaloosa 115

Henrietta MacGuire, Birmingham 123

Marie Stokes Jemison, Montgomery 129

Rose M. Sanders, Mobile 135

Martin Hames, Birmingham 141

Sue Walker, Mobile 145

Marie F. Gillespie, Fairfield 147

Ralph Hammond, Valley Head 155

Frank Theodore Kanelos, Birmingham 163

Irma R. Cruse, Hackneyville 167

Mark Childress, Monroeville 177

Notes on Contributors 181

INTRODUCTION

The purpose of this book is to capture the past and make it live again. After all, Alabama's past is living in everyone who was born in or grew up in Alabama. Yet where are the records? They're in attics, cellars, drawers, boxes . . . and in memories.

In asking 32 Alabamians to unpack their memories, we were hoping to gather some of these jewels that are stored away; to repackage them for sharing. If we could only get people to write about what it was like for them growing up in Alabama, we thought, maybe those who stumble across this book might identify with a passage and not feel so different or alone. Like stumbling across a scrapbook that places you suddenly in the continuum of time. Maybe a few people might say yes, I remember too. And maybe a few might be inspired to record their own stories.

From Tuscumbia to Mobile our authors responded to the idea of *An Alabama Scrapbook* with enthusiasm. People from all kinds of backgrounds and all walks of life were eager to share what made them laugh, what made them cry, what drove them away from Alabama, what brought them home; what made them the people they are today.

We owe a large measure of thanks to the mothers of our authors, who plundered their attics in search of photographs.

We certainly hope authors and mothers (both of whom have been not only cooperative but patient) will be pleased with the results. And above all, we hope that you will find a gem here to stir your own heart.

Ellen Sullivan
Marie Stokes Jemison
Birmingham, 1988

NELL BRASHER

è è è

Sprott, Alabama

I was twelve. Old enough, Daddy had decided, to cook and keep house during the nine days of Mamma's lying-in in April with her sixth child. I overheard Daddy say this to Mamma one night while they were sitting by the fire after supper. No mention of this coming event was made to us. But my ten-year-old brother Sherman and I knew a few things.

To Daddy's inhuman edict that I could cook and keep house I had no recourse. I did mouth my indignation to Mamma but she just kept humming, "Babylon is fallen," as if she didn't know what I was talking about. Later she said if I'd do a good job (of what she didn't say) she would buy the material to make me a crepe de chine dress.

April arrived and on the morning of the tenth, which was a Tuesday, Mamma whispered something to Daddy right after breakfast. He was all set to burn his kiln that day, but before he left he went to fetch Ada, the negro midwife who lived up the hill. When he got back he told Sherman and me to hitch up the two-horse wagon and make a trip to Uncle Will's store, five miles there and five miles back. He said we could make a list of whatever Mamma needed from the store. Taking Lamar, our three-year-old, he then left for the shop. Margie, eight, and G.W., four, our other sister and brother, were at Grandpa Stone's.

Ada arrived in a few minutes, cardboard bag in hand, and began taking charge. Getting our jackets Sherman and I went to the barnlot.

"Daddy just wants to get us out of the way!" Sherman said, wiping his nose on his sleeve.

We hitched Ike and Napoleon, our horses, to the wagon and set off. A more delightful day for such a trip could hardly be imagined. Sunshine like living gold; woods hung with purple, pink, yellow, and blue besides being snowy with dogwood; fragrance of jasmine and bush honeysuckle garlanding the breeze; butterflies, floating up and down on the crabapple blossom air; birds flashing in the woods, mating and nesting; honeybees and bumble bees gathering nectar from sourwood blossoms.

We noted this spring extravaganza with measurable indifference, having our minds taken up with the business at hand. Now and then the crepe de chine dress would flash before my mind's eye and it was the only gleam of comfort I could find as nine days of slavery loomed before me.

The day we'd simultaneously observed that Mamma was going to have another baby we recoiled with shock, then got off to ourselves and hissed and spewed and expressed to each other how mad we were. There were five children in our family and that, we said, was enough! Since then our indignation had mounted steadily.

We got back home from the store in the middle of the afternoon, having dawdled considerably. Jumping out of the wagon we went rushing into Mamma's room to find her in bed with a new baby on her arm. Ada was bustling around getting ready to leave.

"Day plenty vittles cooked for you'll's supper," she said. "I done cooked em while Mis' Dovie gettin ready to birth dat baby." Her plain talk brought a flush of embarrassment to Mamma's face. We sidled over to Mamma's bed. She turned the cover back. "It's a boy," she said. We saw his perfectly shaped little head, covered with black hair, and we accepted him. He was now our brother. It was a whole new thing since we could see him. Suddenly I felt glad. A gush of importance swept over me. Mamma's in bed and I'm in charge, I thought. The other kids will have to mind me and I'm gonna look like a movie star in that crepe de chine dress. I had decided it would be lilac.

Mamma told Sherman to go to the shop and bring Lamar to the house as soon as he got the horses unhitched and turned into the barnlot. We would have to carry Daddy's supper to him since he couldn't leave the kiln and come to the house to eat as he had done at noon. Eighteen hours were required to burn the pottery to stone and after twelve hourse Daddy had to keep firing constantly to hold the kiln at its peak heat of twenty two hundred degrees.

"Has Daddy seen the baby?" I asked.

"No."

"Dat baby wont born when Mr. Zuma come to de house to eat his dinnah," Ada said. Again Mamma's face flushed at Ada's raw reference to the delicate subject.

"Feed the chickens, Nell," Mamma said abruptly.

As Sherman took out the horses I got corn to shell for the chickes, shelled it, and fed them. My attempts to get the two setting hens, with their cheeping biddies, into coops to close them up for the night failed. The attempt ended with the hens squawking, their broods scattered and me screaming. I went into the house and reported this to Mamma. She said just leave them alone.

"You'll have to cook some fresh cornbread for supper," she said. Daddy would not eat leftover cornbread. "After you build a fire in the stove you can go milk the cow. Then when you get back the stove will be good and hot and you can cook the bread."

"Get me some splinters to build a fire with," I ordered Sherman, just back with Lamar, who was crying to get into Mamma's bed. Mamma said put him up.

"Get the splinters yourself!" Sherman said. "Now don't start fussing," Mamma said. She sounded tired. "Sherman go get the splinters. Nell has to milk the cow." He went for the splinters and threw them across the floor when he got back.

Shaking the ashes through the stove grate I poked in the splinters and piled several sticks of wood on top of them. Then I poured on a little kerosene like Mamma always did and struck a match to it. The fire flared right up and began cracking briskly.

Mamma had taken me to the cowpen with her several times in the preceding weeks and let me take turns milking. Twice before when Mamma went to stay with Grandma Stone, who had been sick, it fell my lot to milk the cow. But my heart was not in it.

The first thing I did upon reaching the cowpen was pick up a long stick and lay the law down to Belle, our cow. She threw up her head and trotted across the pen.

When I got some cottonseed meal and put it in her trough she came to it. Squatting down beside her, every nerve on guard, I splashed the warm water, taken from the iron kettle on the kitchen hearth, at her udder and started squeezing. No milk. I kept squeezing. A few squirts.

"You better give that milk down, cow!" I hollered at her. She, eating away, lifted up one of her hind feet and put it back down, then hit me in the face with her tail.

"Oh gosh, I forgot," I said to myself. "The calf has to be let in first so she'll give her milk down." The calf was in a separate pen. I opened the gate.

He made a dash for his ma and began sucking and hunching. After several minutes I tied a rope around his neck, being careful to make a knot that wouldn't slip and choke him, and attempted to pull him off and get him back into his pen until I was finished milking. Then he could have another snack. He was of no mind to let go.

By hard pulling I got him a few feet away from the cow. He tore out around the pen while I, holding onto the rope, feet barely touching the ground, screamed damnation. This happened twice before I succeeded in getting him back into his pen.

Belle then gave down her milk but only stintingly, for I came to the house with two quarts of milk where Mamma brought a gallon. The fire in the stove had gone out.

We were an hour late getting Daddy's supper to him and the cornbread was short on soda. He didn't say a word, though he usually cursed when a meal was late, and he abominated bread without more than enough soda.

The night was chilly. After supper we sat by the small bright fire in Mamma's room. The Sears Roebuck catalog lay unopened in my lap. I was too tired to read yet again the description of the crepe de chine material.

All gladness had left me. After washing the supper dishes alone, including the pots and pans, being in charge had lost its allure. There was no thought of Sherman helping me. He had fed the horses, chopped and brought in wood, and made the fire in Mamma's room. Utterly aside from all that, however, boys didn't wash dishes. I thought of touching him with the dish cloth but felt too weary to hold my own in the fight that would ensue. Sherman considered a dish cloth to be poison. The days of Mamma's lying-in loomed before me like an impassable mountain.

Mamma asked us to leave the room for a few minutes. We knew she wanted to use the chamber pot under her bed but to say that would have been painfully embarrassing to all of us. When we came back into the room, Mamma was sitting propped up against the headboard of the bed. She said, "Hand me the Bible."

I gave it to her. Opening it she began reading with only the firelight and the light from a kerosene lamp on the dresser across the room for illumination. She read briefly, to herself, then handed the Bible back to me and I put it on the mantel.

After this Mamma called for a hippen, lifted the baby across her lap and changed him. This finished she lay down, turned onto her side and put the baby to her breast. In a few minutes we knew by her deep even breathing she was asleep. Lamar was already asleep on the other side of the baby. Daddy would transfer him to either mine or Sherman's bed when he came to the house at midnight, after the kiln was finished firing and sealed.

I went to bed and cried. I didn't want to be in charge. I wanted Mamma to be in charge. In the woods around our house the whippoorwills were calling and, though I usually loved to hear them, tonight their plaintive calls seemed to be the very essence of despair. Sleep, however, was not long in coming and I slept without dreams.

Ada came down the next morning to bathe the baby, whom Daddy had named Jerry Beaman, and to see about Mamma. Coming into the room I heard Ada say, "I'm gwi put dem scissors under yo mattress to cut dem after pains."

This flew all over me. "Ain't a thing to putting them dam scissors under your mattress," I said. Mamma shamed us for using profanity but we were not afraid of her. She never cursed.

"Nell, be ashamed of yourself!" she scolded.

"It's just an old fogie idea!" I snapped. "Daddy don't believe in any of that stuff."

"Yo Pa ain't never had no after pains," Ada said, bristling, "An' neither is you, child! Git on outen heah and leave yo Ma be. I'se seein' after her!"

I got out, sneaking the scissors off the dresser as I left. Ada never did find them.

Nine days came and went. I cooked and kept house but earned no laurels. Roberta, Mamma's unmarried sister, brought Margie and G.W. home and did the family wash. I informed Margie that she could milk the cow once a day. She immediately appealed to Mamma.

"Nell," Mamma said, "what on earth has got into you? You know Margie can't milk the cow!"

"Why?"

"She's too little, that's why, and you know it. She's only eight years old."

"I know how old she is."

"Well, I think you do. Now you get a pan and go in the garden and pick a mess of those run-up turnip greens."

"Margie's the pet!" I said, flouncing out of the room.

The food was sometimes late, sometimes half raw, sometimes unseasoned, but we ate it and Daddy was very patient. Once he let me sleep and cooked salmon patties for breakfast. He put so much flour in them we hardly could tell what they were.

I put the dish cloth on Sherman and we fought. I demanded that Margie wash dishes, and she had to stand in a chair to do it. The dishes were not altogether clean but I wiped off what was left on them and we used them anyway.

At night in bed I wept tears of self-pity mixed with tears of grief over being so mean. But the next day I swept under Mamma's bed and took out the ashes in her fireplace because Ada warned against it, saying bad luck was sure to follow if I did.

When she came as she did every day and saw that I'd spurned her warning she rolled her eyes and said, "De debbil gwi snatch up Nell an' make off wid her lessen she stop temptin' God!"

Mamma didn't say much to either Ada or me. She just lay there in bed, scolding me mildly, agreeing with Ada when Ada was around, looking worried a little, sleeping a lot and humming, "I must tell Jesus."

As soon as Mamma was up again our world fell back in place. The new member of our family quickly became a personality in his own right, and we scarcely remembered having so fiercely resented his coming to join us.

I got the lilac crepe de chine dress.

JOHN FORNEY

Tuscaloosa, Alabama

My uncle, Richard Foster, became president of the University of Alabama in 1935, succeeding Dr. George Denny, who had headed the school for 20 years. The trustees' choice was something of a surprise since Dick Foster was a lawyer, not an educator. Among others who counseled the trustees in their search for a president was Nicholas Murray Butler of Columbia University, and his description of the sort of man they should get fit Dick Foster to a T. The choice, an extremely popular one, was hailed editorially all over the state. Dick had an undergraduate degree from Alabama and his LL.B. from Harvard, and came from well-known families who had been part of the Alabama scene for years.

He was a widower, and his former mother-in-law moved into the president's mansion to supervise operations and be a surrogate mother for Dick's only child, my cousin Lida. Not surprisingly, her abrasive personality caused problems with women from Dick's family who lived in Tuscaloosa — specifically my mother and a close spinster relative who worked for the University, Miss Mary Burke. Miss Mary had been the first dean of women at Alabama, and in that capacity had seen fit to eject one of the school's trustees, a prominent citizen from another city, from the college dance for being tipsy, to say the least, and for touching some of the coeds a bit suggestively, to say even less. In the sober light of day, the trustee demanded Miss Mary be fired, and only the firm intercession of Dr. Denny kept this from happening. In a compromise, she was replaced as dean, but served many years as librarian of the Medical School and today, two coed dorms on the campus bear her name.

Tuscaloosa was a marvelous place in which to grow up, and as the University president's nephew I enjoyed special "perks." These included being able to go to all the football practices (even those closed ones during Tennessee week), and fifty-yard-line seats to all the Crimson Tide games. Coach Thomas and his staff of Hank Crisp, Paul Burnum, Red Drew, Happy Campbell, and especially a tough, ruggedly handsome young coach named Paul Bryant were my idols. I made all of the sports contests that happened on the campus, and also attended many lectures and performances at Morgan Hall. Probably I had a certain status because of kinship with Dick Foster, but I wasn't aware of it. I was aware, though, of the esteem in which he was held by townspeople, as well as students and faculty. Although a latecomer to academe, Dick was elected to several high posts with educational organizations, and his work was recognized in a number of professional journals which my mother always showed me with pride.

The Depression scarcely touched us, although we did have a couple of boarders in our large house six or seven blocks from the campus. I coasted into my twelfth year about as carefree as a youngster could be. Then in 1939 my parents separated and divorced, which I'm sure was a major subject of dinner table conversation around Tuscaloosa households for a long time. My father, a doctor, bought a nearby building as his office, and also lived in an upstairs apartment. This was the old Governor's mansion at the corner of Broad Street and Queen City, and is now the University Club, one of the most beautiful structures in the town. My younger brother and I took Sunday breakfast there where the food was delicious and the conversation awkward.

My life really didn't change that much in the trauma, but Miss Mary Burke did move into the house to be with mother. We continued to have the servants and creature comforts of gracious southern living. I remember a couple of men calling on my mother with red roses and candy and resenting them bitterly. It wasn't long before my father became one of the callers, and in less that a year after their separation and divorce, my parents decided to remarry. This was a joyous occasion as I remember it; my father embracing me in a hold of iron in a twilight driveway, then the drive out to the president's mansion. I stayed in the car while dad went in to tell Dick the news.

Miss Mary Burke moved out, vowing never to return to the house again; so instead of Sunday breakfast with my father, there were long Sunday afternoon visits with her at her apartment in Manly Hall. She was like a grandmother to me, and I have happy memories of her telling me about Perseus and the Golden Fleece and the prodigious labors of Hercules.

While all of this was going on, the world entered another war and Dick Foster faced different sets of problems in guiding the University. Also, he had begun to court a young lady in Tuscaloosa. (Needless to say, single and widowed ladies from all over Alabama had been very attentive to Dick at large and small social occasions.) She was attractive and from a well-known family, but she was a Catholic, and in the year 1941 for the trustees of a Bible-belt state school, this was a distressing occurrence. Having seen them one night sitting close together as Dick's silver gray Packard passed, I had an inkling that it was serious. I was all for it, but had no knowledge of the gravity of the consequencs generated by the religious situation.

My parents were very supportive of the romance, and unquestionably sympathetic about the added pressures placed on Dick Foster. My father told me later that Dick had come close to resigning from the office, and still had it under consideration when he went to Chicago to speak at a large education conference. He came to our house when he returned and told my mother and father how tired he was and that he planned to turn in early. Concerned about him, my mother called the next morning and was told that Dick still felt bad, and was staying in bed. Later that day he called my father and told him he had difficulty in moving some of his limbs, and was barely able to get out of bed.

My father went to the president's mansion and immediately saw that Dick Foster was ill, extremely ill, with some form of fast-moving paralysis. (Lou Gehrig of the Yankees had died shortly before from a similar disease.) He was moved to a room at Druid City Hospital, and my father wasted no time in ordering an iron lung, a relatively little known device, which took over the body's check functions, in effect "breathing" for the patient. The news of Dick's grave illness was all over Tuscaloosa long before the daily newspaper came out.

Hospital officials cordoned off part of a wing for Dick Foster and kept rooms across the hall for family members to stay in vigil or to rest and nap. My father never left Dick's side, before or after the arrival of the iron lung. Miss Mary Burke, who had moved from our house in anger, in her deep concern and appreciation was moved to offer him forgiveness for his previous transgressions as she waited in the family rooms across the way.

I was at the hospital when the machine was hooked up and began to function. Bummm-shhhh, bummmmshhhh. The sound of the lung's contractions and releases dominated the hallway. Once it was working, my father seemed to relax and was hopeful about Dick's chances. There was always a crowd in the family rooms. Tuscaloosans came to call as they would at a sick house, bringing beaten biscuits and ham, deviled eggs and pimento cheese, containers of coffee and sweet rolls. Their goodness and care motivated this, I am sure. But there was also much talk of the iron lung machine, a first for Tuscaloosa. They wanted to see it, or at least hear the bummmmSSShh, bummmSSSHH sounds emanating from it, so dominant were they over the whole hospital floor.

Dick's condition did seem to improve and family members went in one by one. My mother reached in the machine, and Dick was able to give her hand a little squeeze. My father insisted that I go in — I did not want to. I sort of waved at Dick, and I could see an answering smile in the little mirror above his head.

I kept going to Tuscaloosa High School, and stayed at home with two servants and my younger brother as both my parents remained on the "watch" at Druid City Hospital. One morning a messenger from the principal's office came into my English classroom and told the teacher I was wanted in the office. I remember very well the distressed look on the teacher's face, and the quick silence that came over the class, testimony to the awareness of everyone in the town of Dick Foster's illness. The principal met me outside her office and walked through the front door with me, saying that the hospital had called and Dr. Foster's condition had worsened, so she was driving me there.

The bummmSSSHH, bummmSSSHHH greeted me as I walked up the wide hospital staircase, but there was a muffled sound of weeping in the family rooms. I tried to stay near my cousin Lida, and to think of funny things to say or do, hoping to cheer her. My father came in periodically and spoke softly to the people in the room.

Late that day after one of his visits, he saw me and called me over. "Johnny," he said, and I was shocked at the tiredness in his voice — he normally had enormous energy. "How about going across to Druid Drugs and get me a couple of packs of Camels?"

Happy to somehow be serving, I hurried the block or two to the drug store and then back to the hospital. Taking the steps two at a time, I felt something was different. The linoleum covered steps felt the same, the familiar hospital smells were the same, but I realized there was no bummmSSSHHH, bummmSSShhh. Only a terrible new silence. Through the cloth-covered screens which were masking that part of the wing, I could see the backs of hospital attendants as they placed a burden — I knew what it was — on a stretcher and gurney, as my father stood by, his attitude one of total dejection. He saw me and came to the screens. I handed him the cigarettes which he took offhandedly, and put an arm around me. "We lost him, Johnny," he said. "I don't know that we ever had a chance."

People began to come out of the family rooms and leave in various stages of grief and dishevelment. We drove Lida back to the president's mansion past clusters of sombre, sympathetic students. Somehow the carillon of Denny Chimes had been programmed and notes of soft, melancholy songs rolled out over the campus in the chill November air. My mother was telling Lida that she would come and live with us, and I realized then that someone else would be living in the president's mansion and that there would be other changes. I remember a sky full of stars as I stood on the front porch thinking it was the end of something for me, but really it was the end of something for most people on the campus; Pearl Harbor was less than three weeks away.

Dick Foster, dead at 46, had brought the university out of the Depression. Others would carry it forward now.

ELLA LOVELACE

❧ ❧ ❧

Marion, Alabama

Marion — April 9, 1865

The past week has been one of unparalleled excitement in our little town. Yesterday, Saturday evening a week ago, we were at church, the sermon had just commenced, when one of the members of the church went up to the pulpit and whispered something to Mr. Mangham, which of course caused a stir in congregation, and "Yankees, Yankees" was whispered around. Mr. Mangham then dismissed the congregation informally, and we put off for home immediately. I could not help being amused at Ada, wringing her hands and crying, "Oh, I do wish Cousin Charlie was here."

The cause of the alarm proved to be the arrival of a Courier with the news that the enemy were at Centerville, 28 miles above us, and marching directly on this place. Now that it is all over I can laugh at the excited state we were all in. Men galloping through the streets at full speed, wagons rattling by carrying off meat, trunks, etc. The men making for the woods, and the frightened women at home hiding silver, jewelry, clothes, etc. We did not take off our clothes at all that night, but kept watch, and a miserable night it was, for we confidently expected the Yankees before daylight. But day broke, the sun rose, and still no blue coats were in sight. All during the day, it was Sunday, though you would never have known it, the Couriers still galloped in bearing the same news to the groups of excited negroes, women and children on the streets and at the windows. We were all dressed to meet them, which means that each had on three or four chemises, as many underskirts, and stockings without number, and underneath the whole, enormous pockets slung around the waists, and far from empty. Before night, however, the good news came that General Jackson had met that column of the enemy, whipped them and sent them flying across the Cahaba. It was a relief indeed, and with thankful, grateful hearts we lay down to sleep that night. The next day brought confirmation of the news, and Tuesday brought General Jackson and his men, just from the conflict.

In the meantime Forrest had been fighting the enemy all down the Alabama and Tennessee Rivers Railroad and Sunday evening he fell back on Selma, the enemy pressing him closely as to reach there nearly at the same time. Some resistance was made, but it was ineffectual, and the city fell into their hands. General Forrest made his escape with his escort, and most of the men captured have since escaped. Forrest then concentrated his men here and is now on the railroad between Selma and Demopolis. The loss of Selma is a terrible blow to the Confederacy. It was the best of the most important works in the Confederacy, except those at Richmond. Many are the conjectures as to what will be the next move on the part of the enemy, but they are only conjectures. We are shut out from communications with any other place, and know nothing. I heard that General Forrest said he would be obliged to abandon this country, that he could not hold it. If so it will cause the evacuation of Virginia, because the army there is dependent on this State, almost entirely out of supplies. Everything looks dark, but I cannot give up yet. I must still believe and hope that God will give us Independence and Peace, though the day may be far in the future, and we yet be subjected to trials and sorrows.

Marion — May 29, 1865

Another eventful month has passed since I last wrote here. Soon after writing I went out to Mr. John Walthall's and made a long visit of three weeks, only returning last Monday. His house was full of company all the time, and after the quiet life I've led for the last few months, I enjoyed it much. I made some delightful acquaintances whose names I desire to record here that I may not forget them. Col. and Lieutenant Martin, cousins of the Lyons, very pleasant gentlemen. Three Tennesseans made that their headquarters also. Major Cheairs and Captain Ewing just from northern prisons, and Col. Wade, one of the noblest men I ever met . . . He is a very hightoned gentleman, intelligent, highly cultivated, a gallant, brave soldier, possessing noble, warm impulses, and a higher appreciation and estimate of women than you often see nowadays. We spent some delightful hours together and I felt really sorry at parting with him when he left last Sunday for his distant home, after having been in exile for four long years. Years fraught with suffering mental and physical, and devoted to our country's cause. He has been three times wounded and is now on crutches, and it is like reading fiction to hear him tell of some of his narrow escapes. Oh how sad that a ship so nobly defended should at last sink. He gave me a glimpse of his heart history one night, and sad as it is he is yet cheerful, buoyant, the life of every crowd, forcing you to be merry with his good natured witticisms. They all said they were going to tell Captain Lovelace how Col. Wade and I carried on, but no one will tell him more than I, for it isn't often I meet with a gentleman who understands and appreciates me as he did, or that I am so delighted with. We had another pleasant visitor, General George Johnston, an intelligent, ambitious man, but unassuming, pleasant in his manners and a dear lover of music. He would sit and make me play for him by the hour, enjoying it as few do. He is a splendid chess player and I did my very best to beat him, but only occasionally could I gain a game. His life has been saddened by the loss of a noble, lovely wife, and though cheerful the shadow is still there.

I must tell also of a kinsman I found, Col. Hill of Tennessee. A very nice gentleman who represented his district in Congress for a number of years. My visit was a delightful one. The family were kind, even affectionate, and the society gathered there was so congenial and agreeable. They entertain a great deal and do it well, making everybody feel honored and yet at home, and that too with seemingly so little exertion. While there, Grierson with seven thousand men passed near us on his way to Mississippi, via Greensboro. Three stragglers made us a visit trying to take the horses, but found too many officers there and the negroes too faithful. We had quite a laugh at General Johnston's expense of which I cannot stop to tell.

When I returned I found the 9th Minnesota garrisoning the town, and I cannot express my feeling when I see men with hands imbued in the noblest blood of our land, quietly walking our streets, conquering enemies.

Yes since I last wrote, in less than one short month the whole fabric of our Confederacy has fallen to the ground. With the surrender of General Lee's army, unavoidable, cut off from supplies, and surrounded on all sides by nearly five hundred thousand men as it was, the foundation and stay of the Confederacy was gone. His handful of men, after evacuating Richmond, fought five days without a morsel of food, inflicting a terrible wound on Grant's army, killing and wounding nearly 100,000 men. Alas! It was but the death throe. The terrible Anaconda with its slimy folds has at last "crunched the rebellion." Our Generals prisoners, our soldiers disarmed, our President captured, our land desolated, our people broken-spirited, we are at the mercy of our enemies, waiting for but a few more strokes from that gigantic merciless hand to effect our utter annihilation as people. Oh God that it should come to this. That our brave, noble soldiers sleeping beneath the bloodstained battle fields of Virginia, limping through the land on crutches, or with empty sleeves and sightless eyes, should be branded throughout all future history as "Traitors" and "Rebels." Is it not enough to wring the hearts of widows and orphans that all in vain have they given up their loved ones for "heroes in the strife." Oh could we but have gained our independence!

JESSE HILL FORD

❧ ❧ ❧

Jasper, Alabama

Bird dog puppies piled on top of each other in the kennel next to the coal house in the back yard. Next to the kennel the cow pen with Old Bossy and her calf. In the yard with me, Foxy, the old terrier, lame in his left hind leg, patiently following, keeping me out of trouble. On the walk in front of the house Uncle Breck, strolling up and down with the help of his cane.

Uncle Breck is Colonel Breckenridge Musgrove to others, and has built a church of finest Italian marble not far from Jasper's public square where the Confederate Soldier stands on his pinnacle above the gatherings of the many wagons, mule drawn, and the many automobiles — some with rumble seats. Uncle Breck does not attend the church, having been evicted some years earlier for the sin of dancing.

He has also given the Golf and Country Club, thus providing on the one hand a place in which to sin and on the other hand a temple in which to repent — what more could be expected of Uncle Breck? He also gave my uncle the dog, Foxy, the faithful old terrier.

In the kitchen the black cook, Bessie, scalds and plucks a chicken. One room away Mrs. Mooney, my grandmother's white help, is ironing and speaking both plaintively and wistfully of her son who is away in prison for something.

"I tell you, Miss Pearl," says Mrs. Mooney to my grandmother. "Little Frank, he's plumb pretty."

My grandfather reads the newspaper. He peels apples for me. My grandmother rocks me to sleep every afternoon and sings lullabies to me and her hair is blonde, the color of yellow smoke, and her eyes are blue. In winter she wears a coat my grandfather brought her from New York, with a great white fur collar, and in the fur some suggestions of yellow, like the smoke from leaves before they burst into flame, and the collar is like her beautiful hair.

Barney, my uncle, and the oldest son, plays center for Walker County High. Barney is a football star. He drinks lots of milk. I drink my milk. I want to be like Barney. Rossie, the younger son, is the neighborhood leader at thirteen and goes away with the gang of boys to hunt turtles in Town Creek. I want to be like Rossie. The captured turtles swim around and around in the big wash tub.

My father wakes up in the night, hearing the sounds of the turtles. He creeps out with his shotgun, sure that someone must be in the coal house, stealing coal — but it is only the sound of the turtles rattling against the sides of the tub.

Some days a wagon will stop in Florida Avenue before the big white clapboard house. The driver will set the brake. The mules will stand patiently. The farmer is selling fresh corn, tomatoes, squash, string beans, live chickens. If my grandfather will take me out to the man's farm I can see the goats, the farmer promises — a big man wearing brogan shoes and bib overalls, with red cheeks and a straw hat and a blue bandanna handkerchief. He chews tobacco.

And there is the ice wagon. The driver gives me a sliver of ice which has the taste of the wooden bed of the wagon about it.

When the cow is milked late in the afternoon I'm given some of the milk, warm from the cow, not like any other milk — warm and with a different taste, and the smell of the stall, of cow feed, and Bossy eating and the milk streaming against the pail with a thin sound. Barney milks the cow and has strong fingers. The teats have to be washed first, and the side of the cow like a wall, huge and warm and Bossy shakes her head, eating.

Near the square downtown are my grandfather's dry goods store and the Peoples Drug Company where my father fills prescriptions. The porter at the Peoples Drug Company is young, very muscular, and very black, and he walks about whispering to himself, unaware that I, as small as I am, can hear him, whispering, chanting to himself: "Fucka, fucka, fucka." I have no idea what it means, what he says. "Fucka, fucka, fucka." It must be something very special, I decide.

On the sidewalk beside the Peoples Drug Company two stalwart, feuding citizens of Jasper gunned each other down one day. Oh, the stories, the accounts of the shooting, the confrontation, the causes of the grudge, a good if tragic and most interesting story.

And across the square the Burton Manufacturing Company which once made harnesses and now makes golf bags. The Burtons are neighbors on Florida Avenue and Rossie Musgrove and Pat Burton string a line between the two houses to make a telephone and shout:

"Can you hear me, Pat?"

"Can you hear me, Rossie?"

The phone never quite works. Oh, well . . .

Yes, I remember Alabama.

REVEREND SOLOMON S.SEAY, SR.

❧ ❧ ❧

Shorter, Alabama

I was born on a plantation in Macon County on January 25, 1899. My parents were tenants. Every year after the crops had been gathered in, usually there was nothing left for the tenants, so far as things for their children at Christmas time.

Usually the tenants went to the merchant to get something for their children for Christmas. My mother — who was in charge of farming at that time — went, and it just happened that one year I went with her. I don't remember my age but I must have been five or six years old. Early in the morning she arrived at the place and stayed there all day, waiting an opportunity to ask the merchant about what she could get for her Christmas — I was playing around on the floor but I could always tell my mother had grave concern and was rather apprehensive. She'd fold her arms and have a frown on her face.

Way in the afternoon she went to the merchant and said to him, said, "Mr. Pinkston" — and some of the Pinkstons are here now, in this city — "do I get anything for my children for Christmas?"

And of course he said, "Yes, Hagar." He said, "You one of my good tenants and I will give you something." And whatever he gave her, she got some li'l toy pistols, li'l jews harps, and li'l stuff to make some cake and custards.

But as a child, that really did something to me. My mother saw to it that Christmas didn't happen that way anymore.

She raised turkeys and planted peas and whipped them out, and had the bigger boys to chop cord wood. And at Christmas time after that she would drive those 21 miles from Shorter to Montgomery, and sell that stuff on the street. And that's how she bought what she needed for her children for Christmas.

VIRGINIA FOSTER DURR

❧ ❧ ❧

Union Springs, Alabama

Visits to Grandmother Foster on the Union Springs Plantation at Christmas and summer were the anticipated pleasures of our childhood years. To run free across fields, free of elaborate city clothing, to play day and night with my young black friends was my idea of heaven on earth. I adored this grandmother for whom I was named, who took us less seriously than Mother did.

The old North-South railroad, which later became the Louisville and Nashville, left for the southern part of the state early in the morning. First came the depot dray for the trunks. Then the depot hack for the riders. Sally the cook was left in charge of Daddy, who could only spare a week in summer and a few days at Christmas away from his pastoral duties in Birmingham. Nursie went with us.

The trip to Montgomery ninety miles away was long and tiresome, dirty, gritty, and smoky. The train reached Montgomery in time for 1:00 dinner, which was taken at the Exchange Hotel. The next lap to Union Springs was on the Central of Georgia Railroad. Lagging spirits picked up as the last stops were made at Pike Road, Matthews Station, Midway, Mt. Meigs, Peachburg, Fitzpatrick, and at last — Union Springs! As children and luggage spilled from the train, there waiting for us, his high hat shining, his horses sparkling, would be Wash, Grandmother Foster's driver.

As we drove up to the steps of the old white columned house, Easter stood on the porch and Grandmother just inside the door. Easter had been a slave, and nobody knew her age. Small and coal black, she wore a spotless, starched white dress apron and head handkerchief. A person of immense dignity, she held herself erect and with authority. We knew she ran the house because she wore the keys. We children were scared to death of her, but we loved her devotedly. She was absolutely fair. We used to think she had eyes in the back of her head. I'm sure that one of the reasons I couldn't believe blacks were "inferior" was because I had the example of Easter all my young life. Although she could neither read nor write, she ran the business of the plantation, she even ran her mistress, Grandmother.

Virginia Heard Foster, my grandmother, was still a pretty woman in her late seventies. She had traces of red in her hair and bright blue eyes, and she never seemed old to us. She married at fifteen and bore fifteen children, the last when she was fifty-four. By 1908 only four were left. But she didn't act as if she'd had a sad life. She was like a queen bee with lots of honey to give away. She had absolutely nothing to do except what she wanted. Old Easter slept at the foot of her bed, and bathed and dressed "Miss Ginny" every day. Granny had little or no education, never read magazines or newspapers, yet she was utterly charming and everybody adored her.

Granny's days had a regular routine. After she was bathed and dressed in the morning, she would come down to a huge breakfast, full of plans for the day: someone to go and see, some shopping, perhaps preparations for company. All morning she sat in the morning room and received visitors or played Finch with us children. She never hesitated to make the game more exciting by cheating. If she was caught, she would throw back her head, laugh and say, "Ah ha, you caught me," in the best of humor. After an enormous mid-day dinner, she took a nap, bathed, and dressed again to go out for a drive or to visit the shops.

Granny had the reputation of being a great lady. I remember one day I asked my mother what made someone a lady. She thought hard; she always tried to answer my questions seriously. "Darling," she replied slowly, wrinkling her pale brow. "A lady is one who does not have to do her own washing."

The treatment Granny received from the proprietors of the dry goods store or the butcher shop was evidence of her rank in society at Union Springs. She never got out of her carriage to enter a store. The owners brought their wares to her. Cozy in her satin-lined coach on a chilly day, she made her selections of linen and lace or a fresh-killed pig. The linen she bought in large quantities, for she had all of our clothes made in Union Springs. Miss Katie and her two old maid sisters did the exquisite hand embroidery on our dresses, underwear, and coats. Our bonnets were bought at the dry goods store, but Miss Katie often added a ribbon or flower. The sisters had lost everything in the war, and the people of Union Springs thought Granny so kind to provide them with work.

The Birmingham ladies of Highland Presbyterian Church thought otherwise. I remember one of the ladies meeting me on Highland Avenue, walking with my nurse. She turned me upside down to look at my drawers and sniffed, "Real lace on a child's drawers! How absurd. Personally, I like my preachers to be a little humble."

At Union Springs our routine almost matched that of home, with the exception of family prayers. Only Daddy's short visits reinstated this ceremony; Granny didn't care much for the added ritual. Sunday church was a different matter. Wash, more shined up than ever, would come around in the coach or surrey and we children in our ribbons and bows followed Grandmother inside. In winter she wore long flowing taffeta dresses, usually black, with a bonnet trimmed in jet. In summer, the gown was long but of pastel voile and her bonnet wore flowers. The minister waited for her arrival on the curb. Even at four and five, somehow I knew that the Reverend Bell was Her preacher, and the church was Her church, and that she owned both. Of course she did, because she was the largest contributor.

Christmas season in the Black Belt was the hunting season. Hunting was the chief pastime for men in the rural South and the season was anticipated all year. At Christmas, the plantation house overflowed with our family, sometimes Father's sister May and her family from New York, and Father's brothers Robert and Hugh and their families.

After a hearty early breakfast on the day of the hunt, the Foster brothers and their guests shouldered their rifles, mounted their horses, and with much bravado rode off for the kill. At mid-day they returned with shouting and hullabaloo, the dogs nipping and barking at the heels of the horses drawing the wagon filled with the day's catch. Before 1:00 dinner, the family gathered in the parlor to hear tall tales as the hunters warmed themselves before the fire.

On the back porch, the black beaters who had attended the gentlemen cleaned birds and told their version of the hunt.

On Christmas Day, Grandmother Foster entertained the whole town with eggnog and fruit cake, and under the big cedar tree lay small presents for everyone in Sunday School. After the towns-people left, the black children were invited to come in for refreshments and presents. I always thought Grandmother showed great imagination in selecting presents. Once I remember she gave a small player piano to one of the black children and I begged to swap. But Grandmother stood over the child saying sternly, "Don't you let her take it away from you. It is yours."

As soon as we'd left the plantation after our Christmas visit, all we could think about was going back for summer. Summer was even more anticipated than winter; I remember long, hot airless days that seemed to stretch out forever. I would wake in the morning to the sound of tinkling cowbells and the heavy, sweet scent of wisteria and honeysuckle floating in my open window. Creeping out of the dark bed where mother lay sleeping, I would go downstairs to find Nursie and get dressed. As soon as breakfast was over we would go out back, collect our playmates, and the games started. We made doll houses in the roots of the ancient live oaks and dolls from corn shucks. The boys were allowed to ride horses and chase bulls, but this was a privilege reserved for males. I remember throwing a fit of anger at Grandmother's when I could not go and see the calf born. I was told little girls were not supposed to see things like that, only boys.

The plantation overflowed with abundance during those inno-cent years. Chickens, sheep, cows, beef cattle, ducks and geese roamed the place. Every variety of flower and vegetable flourished, and pans of rich clabber lined the back porch. Easter bossed dozens of Negroes who did it all. Little children were plentiful on the plantation, but there were also some very old men and women who sat in the sun and smoked pipes. Former slaves who did not choose freedom, they lived in cabins in the backyard and did not work at all. Granny used to tell us tales of slavery days. She told us how much better off the colored people were in those days when the white people looked after them as she did. Now they had no one to nurse them when they were sick or look after them when they were old.

Toward the end of my fifth summer, as the black folk used to say, "a rabbit done run over the grave." Something strange and unexplainable happened. All the children, black and white, loved my sister Josephine and called her Sis. One morning we all went around to the front porch where the Foster women were rocking. One little black boy within earshot of the rockers called, "Come over here, Sis, come here." The children crowded around him as he tried to make a toad jump over a stick. Later, as the heavy noontime heat slowed the playmates and we lounged lazily on the back steps, chewing on straws, old Easter came out looking more solemn than usual. She addressed the children directly as was her custom. "You black chillun listen to me. You can't call Sis Sis anymo'. You got to call her Miss Josephine. She is too ole for you to call her Sis. Miss Ginny says so and don't you let me heah you calling her Sis no mo'."

I was bewildered. "Can't I call her Sister?" I asked Easter.

"You know I was talking about these black chillun. They got to know better than to call her Sis," answered Easter gruffly and she went inside.

The little group sat in silent shock. We didn't understand, but we felt threatened. Easter's word was law. Finally Josephine stood up and looking with her sweet, sad expression at the children, said "I tell you what. You just call me Miss Sis. I think that would be all right." From then on, to everyone of the plantation, Josephine was known as Miss Sis.

RICHARD ARRINGTON, JR.

҉ ҉ ҉

Livingston, Alabama

I was born in Sumter County, Alabama, on October 19, 1934, and lived there — outside the town of Livingston — until I was about four or five years old. I have one brother who is also a biologist, who now lives in South Carolina.

When I was four or five, my father decided to move his family to Birmingham. My father was a sharecropper; he worked for a family by the name of Nixon. Leland Nixon the man's name was — he's a man my mother and father are still very close to and fond of. In fact, they hardly go home to Livingston to visit without going back to see Mr. Nixon.

My father lived on Mr. Nixon's land, which was really called "Bell's Place." My mother comes from the Bell family, and a lot of people, I know most of the blacks in that area, thought the Bells owned all that land. We never actually owned any of the land, however. It was called Bell's Place because my mother's family grew up there, and a large number of my uncles lived there. What happened was that when my great-great grandfather on my mother's side was growing up — he was about three years old when slavery was abolished — there was a family that owned this land who were very fond of him. And they turned all the land over to him to live on.

Eventually, the Nixons purchased some of the land, so we ended up sharecroppers for the Nixon family. And there may have been another family involved, I can't recall. But I do remember Mr. Nixon.

As is usually the case with sharecropping, you work year in and year out; you never get out of debt. No matter how good the crop is you still owe the man. I remember that much — and I do have some other memories of what the farm was like, even though I was only four or five when we left. I did go back a number of summers, too, to visit my grandparents.

I recall at a very young age working in the field. I didn't do very much, but I did have a sack for picking cotton. And I had the responsibility, even at that age, of running water to the field for the workers. I would have to go to the spring, which I guess was the equivalent of eight or ten city blocks from where we lived. I can still see it vividly: the horses drank from one side and we got water from the other side. And I'd bring buckets of water from the other side. And I'd bring buckets of water to the field for my parents and aunt and some uncles who were working.

We lived about 12 or 15 miles outside Livingston. We had large fields of melons, corn, and cotton. And I remember well that the inside walls of our house were papered with old Sears and Roebuck catalogs. The windows were just board windows — open windows. There was a barn out back, and we had a couple of mules and a horse. My father had a blacksmith shop; he was also a blacksmith. He was a very talented man, although he had very little formal training. He went through third grade in a country school. For blacks, I guess that was representative of the worst available education. As he tells it, all the grades were in one room.

Although he only went for three years, he was as I said very gifted. He was a carpenter, too; he built quite a few homes down in Sumter County. He did all of the maintenance work for the Nixon farm. He did all the shoeing of horses in addition to farming. And even in Birmingham, while he was working at the steel mill, he was building homes. There are a number of homes in the Fairfield area that were built by my father.

Another early memory of those days is taking the horse down to water, and the difficulties I had trying to get back up on him after getting down! There was no saddle or anything.

But one of the strongest recollections of my childhood is the emphasis my parents put on education. On my mother's side in particular. My great-great grandmother was an educator, and in fact most of the Bell family taught. They didn't finish college, but most of them went off to school. One uncle went to Tuskegee and he stayed I think a year and a half. And another one went to A&M for a year or so. They came back and taught and were looked up to as educators.

I remember, before I was old enough to attend school, going to school with my grandmother a number of times. She taught in a little church not far from where we lived. And she was a strict disciplinarian. I remember how difficult it was for me to sit there and pay attention; she insisted that we pay close attention.

I suppose, in Livingston, we were poor but I didn't know it. And I suppose we were poor after we moved to Birmingham, but I didn't know that either.

One day in 1938 or 1939, my father decided he wanted to seek a better life for his family — to seek his fortune in the steel mills in Birmingham. He didn't have the money to come up and get a job, but he had several brothers working in steel mills. So he wrote one of them, I think it was my Uncle Elvis, and borrowed the bus fare. He came to Birmingham and got a job in the Fairfield area working at the wire mill.

Shortly after that, he came back in his brother's car and moved our whole family to Birmingham.

I should note here that my father had 19 brothers and sisters. Of those, all but one lived to an advanced age — quite a few are still alive today. When my father's mother died, his father married again and they had five more children. I spent a great deal of time with my father. All the children in his family ultimately left farming and went on to different things. Most came to Birmingham. Eventually some moved on to Chicago and other places.

I remember how excited I was when we left in a car to come to Birmingham. I'd never been any place outside of Livingston before. The one trip I had taken was the trip to town on Saturdays. My Dad and I would hitch up the wagon on Saturdays and go downtown. We didn't do much of anything downtown — we'd purchase a few items. But basically, you just sat around — black sat around in one area, white in another — and you just sat there and talked.

So that trip to Birmingham was about the biggest thing that had ever happened to me. We arrived early in the evening, and I remember sitting out on the porch. My father had rented one side of a duplex house. It had three rooms, a living room, bedroom, and kitchen, one right behind the other. Eventually we got a toilet on the back porch, but at that time you only had dry toilets out in the back yard.

I remember first of all the lights of the city. We didn't have electric lights out in the country in Sumter County. We had oil lamps. I was excited about those electric lights, and I remember sitting out on the porch looking at them. And in the distance I could hear a streetcar turning around. Car Number 7 turned around in Vinesville, where we lived. And I thought it was a train, because I had gone through the train station in Livingston and I had seen trains before. I asked my mother if that's what it was, and she said no, it's a streetcar. That was very puzzling to me, because I'd never seen one or even read about one. I had no idea what a streetcar was. I was anxious to get up the next morning so I could look out and see what it looked like.

We lived in the Vinesville/Fairfield area, as I said, and I attended the Fairfield schools. I went from there to Miles College.

So I was the first person in the family to go to college, and I went without any idea of what I wanted to do. All I knew was that I had to go to college because my parents had always said I had to go. Even in elementary school my mother would sit with me and go over my homework; it was very important to her. She used a switch with great frequency. Most of the discipline I received was given out by my mother. In my entire life, my father punished me twice. I remember both times, and I'm glad he only did it twice!

Once when I was in Livingston, and my mother had gone someplace on a Sunday afternoon, I was pulling green peaches from a tree in the yard. My father, who appears to never pay any attention to anything but what he's doing, but seems to see everything, said for me to stop. And I did for a short while. But when I thought he was no longer watching and was busy reading, I started doing it again. I remember he ran off the porch and pulled off a big limb with peaches on it and hit me. After that I never wanted him to whip me again, but it did happen one more time.

It was after we'd moved to Birmingham, and I stole 20 cents from him. He was changing into his work clothes and had laid 20 cents on what we called the mantel — a little shelf over the heater. I was walking by and I took the 20 cents and put it in my pocket and started to walk down the street. By the time I got halfway down the block my dad came out on the porch, and he called me, "Vay, come here."

We all had nicknames during those times; my mother and father called me "Vay." So I went back and he said, "Did you see any money in there?" I said, "No sir, I didn't." He said, "I had some money on the mantel." Again I denied seeing it. He said, "Let me see what you've got in your pocket."

So he went in my pocket and there were the two dimes. He took me into the house then and he stood up against the wall with his razor strap and gave me a good beating. And then he made me take the 20 cents and go on!

I was fortunate because I ended up in a good Fairfield school under a strong educator by the name of A. J. Oliver, who held both students and teachers to high standards. One of the things we were proud of at our school was our performance in the academic meets that were held at Alabama State University. Dr. Oliver, who died around 1980, insisted we do well in all these meets. He was also a strict disciplinarian.

I decided in high school that I wanted to be a dry cleaner. The school was a vocational school. For students planning to go on to college, there was what we called a straight academic program.

Even though I'd been an honor student all the way through school, I followed some of my friends and wanted to go into tailoring. But the class was sealed up. I remember in 10th grade we all went into the auditorium and were expected to make a decision about which trade we wanted to study — or whether to stay in a straight academic program. In my class of 100 or so students, there were only two or three who took the straight academic program: chemistry, math, and so forth.

The school couldn't handle all of us who wanted tailoring. So we put our names in a hat, and I missed out on tailoring. So I decided I wanted to go into dry cleaning. I spent my last two years of high school studying dry cleaning during half of the school day.

It may not have been a complete disaster, because after I graduated and went to Miles College I got a job working in a dry cleaner's on Third Avenue. I worked there for four years, and it paid my way through college.

But as I said, I didn't really know what I wanted to do. I was fortunate to end up at Miles because there was a teacher there, a lady still living, named Burdell Martin. She became interested in me in a psychology class. She sent for me and said she wanted to know what I intended to do with my life. I said I didn't know, and she said, "Well I've been impressed with you and I think you should go talk to a man over in biology, Emmett Jones. I think you have an aptitude for science." Sure enough, I went over and talked to him and that's how I decided to go into biological sciences.

I'd never heard of graduate school. When I was about to graduate, Emmett Jones suggested I consider going on. He contacted his former professor up at the University of Detroit, and that's how I went there. I hadn't been out of Alabama up to this point.

I was married by that time, and I remember leaving for Detroit and how we all cried. Eventually I got a doctorate at the University of Oklahoma. You have to remember that at that time Alabama schools were still segregated by race. When I went to Detroit, and later at Oklahoma, I got a stipend from the state. It was part of a program for blacks who went out of state to school. It paid the difference between what I would have paid if I'd been able to go to Auburn or Alabama, and what it cost me to go out of state. It came to about $300 per term. That was the state's way of trying to maintain the segregated system, yet help pick up some of the expense of education for blacks.

One thing I'll always remember is my first semester at Detroit, and what a traumatic experience it was for me. After all, I'd grown up in Birmingham, which was rigidly segregated then. There was hardly any communication between the races. The only whites I really knew were those I worked for.

There were about 15,000 students at the University of Detroit, with less than a dozen blacks on campus. I ended up at first being the only black in the Department of Biology. I was later joined by a woman who is now a dentist in Alabama.

At that time, if you were black you'd been told all your life, either directly or indirectly, that you were inferior. No matter what people told you or how you fought it off, you had to get to the point where you could gain a sense of your own identity. I guess that point came for me in Detroit.

I did well there, and I was well-prepared for the courses. But I remember sitting in relatively small graduate classes in endocrinology and genetics, and if it was a situation with questions and answers, I felt I had to always know the answer. If I didn't know the answer — even if I knew the answers to four out of five questions I was asked — I felt as if I'd let the whole black race down.

Many of the students there were very friendly and seemed to pay no attention to the fact that I was black. That was very new to me and it took me awhile to adjust to that, and see myself as just a graduate student. But somewhere along the way, maybe just maturity, I gained some sense of my own identity. But I'll always remember the first trauma of a "mixed" racial situation.

I'll also remember forever how badly I wanted to come back to Birmingham. I was so homesick that I used to try to take exams early so I could come home early for vacations.

Even after that, when I went on to other places, other opportunities — Washington University, where I was a National Science Foundation Fellow, the State University of Iowa, Oklahoma, and eventually Harvard — I always missed Alabama. And I always came back to Birmingham.

I always intended to come back.

ALVIS HOWARD

❧ ❧ ❧

Huntsville, Alabama

Nowhere that I have ever gone, nothing that I have ever seen conjures in my memory the joy and delight that I experienced growing up in Huntsville, Alabama. Today, Huntsville has changed. It is a space and rocket and high technology center and it has grown from a small (16,000 population) agricultural town in 1948 to a cosmopolitan city of almost 200,000. People from all over America and the world now make Huntsville their home and little remains of the original city as it once was. Only the downtown area has any remnants of the past. But I can close my eyes at any moment and bring it all back.

I was born right downtown in Huntsville. "Me and Tallulah Bankhead!" I always say, then add, "at different times of course."

I have many early and very vivid memories, back even when I was only three or four years old. We lived in a house across from the Times Building, at the corner of Green Street and Holmes Avenue. There was a picket fence around the yard and each afternoon I used to go to the corner of the fence and step up on the inside bottom rail and hold to the top picket slats and wait for a beautiful redhaired young lady who worked in a drug store on the next corner. Almost every afternoon she brought me a chocolate ice cream cone. There was a cheerful, rotund, elderly man who always wore a big white apron, and who ran a sort of diner a few doors down from our house. I would ride my tricycle around the block and stop in front of his cafe and he would always come out and give me a small glass bottle of chocolate milk. Today when I think of this I can still taste that chocolate milk. No chocolate milk in later years has ever tasted exactly like that.

On the same block was an athletic gym where they held boxing matches. A friend lived in an apartment that had windows on one side that was level with the rooftop of the gym building. He and I used to crawl out on the roof, without our parents knowing, and watch the fights through the skylight. I can still hear the sound of those leather gloves hitting flesh, see those two strange white bodies beneath the bright lights, and smell the sweat, smoke, canvas, and leather.

This was the Depression Era and hard times were everywhere. My family had their share of these, but remembering today, the hard times seem to fade compared to the good memories I have. When I think of my adolescent years, I sometimes have a sadness of almost depressive dimension knowing that my two sons never experienced, nor do many children experience, the kind of contact with real life as I did. No one touches, feels, smells, or sees real things anymore. Everyone lives their lives as if they are prepackaged in plastic wrap. What does a supermarket smell like? Nothing. There is no smell.

I can't imagine a lasting, fond association with a McDonald hamburger, Kentucky Fried Chicken, K-Mart, Krogers, or National Shirt Store. When I was growing up, every store in Huntsville had a name that was instantly identifiable with a real, live human being whom you knew by name. And in most cases you knew their family members as well. You also knew all of the people who worked in these businesses. You saw and spoke to these business people often.

Every business was really unique and had a character of its own. A business succeeded as much on the uniqueness of its owner as on the owner's business acumen. People would speak of these businesses in an intimate manner and relate why "old-so-in-so" was a success. It really helped (in some cases it was almost a necessity) if the owner was somewhat of a legend or had done something that was a legend. No businesses in those days were successful without a certain amount of mystique. If the owner had a shady or colorful background, success was almost instantly assured. For the word of mouth publicity, via the gossip train, alerted the population far and wide that here was as individual that was worth viewing, and the only way that viewing could take place was in visiting the business. The added dividend for the business was that folks back then didn't just expect a quick glance or peek at such a person; a complete and thorough review was required. Thus many prolonged visits to the business were usually required by everyone to completely arrive at an individual appraisal. Obviously this fostered debate which required additional visits, and this chain reaction resulted in the constant ring of the cash register, hence business success.

Ex-bootleggers, prostitutes, ex-convicts, adulterers; someone who had killed someone, preferably with a gun; are all examples of the leading types of backgrounds that would certainly insure the instant success of a business in those days. An example of a common legend was that over half of the businesses in Huntsville were started by people with only two dollars in their pocket. It was for this reason that I never could understand why the two dollar bill was considered so unlucky, since two dollars had been so lucky for so many business people in Huntsville. The downtown area consisted of fourteen square blocks; but the human traffic and main commerce revolved around the courthouse square and along a three block stretch of Huntsville's two main streets, Washington and Jefferson, and along the interconnecting streets of Clinton and Holmes.

I always liked the mornings, when the downtown area was like a circus or County Fair "setting up" for business. Businesses used to have to get set up before opening. Everywhere you looked bread, wholesale grocery, produce, soft drinks, ice, candy, and freight trucks were parked helter-skelter putting in a fresh daily supply of provisions to the multitude of restaurants, drug stores, newsstands, hotels and grocery stores that lined the streets in the downtown area.

Windows were being washed by men and boys using rubber squeegees on long poles. Many colored canvas awnings were being let down to shelter the store fronts from the sun. Sidewalks and business entrances were being mopped, swept, or washed down with hose pipes.

Many groceries had wooden, tray-like counters jutting out in front of the store. These were filled with fresh fruit and vegetables, and there would be bushel baskets of greens and sweet and Irish potatoes, and the ever-present hanging stalk of bananas. Are there any kids today who have ever seen a stalk of bananas?

Businesses also had props; props that were representative of the nature of the business. They either hung out or stood on stands in front of the business. I remember a pair of huge metal boots (shoe repair), eyeglasses (optometrist), steak (restaurant), dollars (loan company), camera (photographer), rocking chair (furniture store), hat (hats blocked), and of course there were the three balls for the pawn shop and many revolving peppermint-striped barber shop poles.

Many stores exhibited their wares right on the street. Clothing stores had metal racks on the sidewalk, hardware stores had farm implements and tools and bicycles arrayed out front.

There were the town characters one always saw in the morning. The ones I remember best sold newspapers. One was called Crazy Bill who looked a lot like Fuzzy Knight the movie cowboy sidekick. He sold the old *Birmingham Age-Herald* newspaper and he twisted his mouth like Crazy Guggenheim when he talked. He had a hump back, and he would sing-song all morning long, "Newsseee Age-Herald! Then he would sort of laugh, "He! Hee!"

Another town character was called Johnny Bell. He walked with a slight stoop and had a perpetual smile on his face and wrote very beautiful religious poetry. He would write an original poem in a matter of minutes in perfect meter. He managed to get a collection of his poems published in a small volume. He called everyone brother. When he sold someone a paper he would say, "Thank you brother."

There was lots of traffic downtown. There were no one-way streets. Traffic traveled two ways on all streets; there was parallel parking along both sides of all streets, except on the courthouse square where the cars parked "headin" around the courthouse itself, and into the street curbs on all four sides of the square. The bus station was located downtown on Washington Street as well as two taxi stands. There were at least ten or twelve gasoline stations and tire stores in the downtown area. There were also two black-smith shops. There were many mule and horse drawn vehicles in the downtown area of Huntsville well into the middle '40s.

I remember very vividly a two-mule wagon "running away" as they called it. The team became wild for some reason down on Meridian Street which entered the downtown area at the foot of Washington Street. There was a battery-repair shop at the corner of Washington and Halsey Alley which intersected Meridian. The team raced up Meridian toward town but rather than negotiating the turn onto Washington, they leaped the curb and went right through the window of the battery shop. I remember the bleeding, panting animals lying on the floor of the shop. A huge crowd gathered and the mules were eventually shot.

There was a night watchman for the downtown area even though the police maintained a foot patrol of the area both night and day. The night watchman's name was Allison and he wore a pearl gray fedora and always had the stub of a cigar clinched in his mouth. He carried a pistol but his most conspicuous piece of equipment was a huge flashlight — it must have been two or three feet long. They called him a "door-shaker" because that was what he did. He would go along the street throughout the entire downtown area and shake all doors to ensure that they were locked. He would also beam his huge flashlight up all alleys to see if anyone was lurking about. Every morning he would have breakfast at the Central Cafe. He would sit there with his big pearl grey fedora on and his cigar clinched in his mouth and his huge flashlight standing beside his chair on the floor while he sipped coffee.

On Washington Street right downtown was a boarding house — Swaim's boarding house. It was located on the second floor of a two-story building. Boarders would sit out front of the building in the morning and afternoon, on the sidewalk, in cane-bottomed chairs. The son of the owners of the boarding house, Roy Swaim, ran a cafe adjacent to the boarding house building. He sold two main items — hamburgers and hot dogs. He had a long counter that ran the length of the cafe. There was a row of stools for the counter. These were the old-fashioned cafe stools with round, backless seats, which you could sit on, and while you were waiting for your order, spin yourself round-and-round. He also had a row of desk-type chairs along one wall of the cafe. These were the kind of chairs that had a small flat surface on one arm about eight or ten inches wide. This was for writing on or, in Roy's case, eating on.

Roy cooked his hamburgers, which were thick and square, in a deep rectangular metal pan which contained about two inches of fat. The hamburgers were actually deep-fried, but were not hard of course, but rather tender and juicy. He put the hamburgers on square buns that were baked fresh daily one block up the street at the Tasty Bakery. He added onions and mustard to crown the hamburgers which were acclaimed far and wide. Roy had a secret recipe for his hamburgers and over the years many people tried to learn the secret but no one ever did. Roy eventually gave up his cafe and opened a grocery store on Meridian Pike next to the Alabama A&M College which he ran for many years. From time to time a newspaper or some other medium would hear a story about Roy Swaim's famous hamburgers and would do a piece on him, but the Swaim Hamburger Secret was never revealed. But there was one thing for certain, anyone who had ever eaten one would tell you that Roy Swaim really had a secret hamburger.

Huntsville had red brick streets up until the late '30s, when the streets were torn up and paved with concrete. I remember walking home from school and stopping to climb up on a huge pile of dirt which was dug up around the courthouse when the paving was going on. A number of large trees had been used to improve the foundation of the courthouse in an earlier time. These trees were uncovered during the paving and had to be removed. It took a large excavation around the courthouse to remove the trees and make a new foundation for the street.

There was a small green-colored peanut stand which stood on the sidewalk on the north side of the courthouse square. It was run by a thin balding man who wore a bill-type World War I soldier hat and sometimes puttees and army shoes. He said he had fought in the Big War overseas (World War I). He cooked spanish-type peanuts in a hopper of grease and sold them in a small brown sack for a nickel each. They tasted sensational. The peanut stand was large enough for him to work inside of it and it was covered with glass on four sides from about halfway up. He ran the stand until well up into the early '40s.

But if ever there were paradises on earth, they were embodied in two institutions of my Huntsville childhood: the dime store and the movie theater, which we all called the "picture show." I and all of the friends I knew had but one paramount and overriding goal in life each week. Nothing — death, famine, flood, war — nothing had priority over this: raising show fare for the weekend picture show, and if at all possible, something for a trip to the candy counter at the dime store.

I have thought about it many times and am completely convinced that neither the movies nor television of today come even close to providing the strange and captivating ambience that pervaded the movie theaters of the late '30s and '40s. It was exciting just to think about the picture show. The transmigration from street to lobby to vestibule to the sanctuary of the theater itself, through thick velvet curtains, was truly spine-tingling. The darkness wrapped around you like a big cotton quilt on a cold night and the glow of the silver screen was as mesmerizing as Rasputin. I sold papers and magazines, kindling wood, scrap iron, wild blackberries and poke salad; I picked cotton and cut wood and lawns to earn picture show fare. Sometimes, but rarely, my Daddy had a little extra and he would pay my way. It cost a dime to get in and you saw a cowboy picture — Roy Rogers, Gene Autry, Ken Maynard, Buck Jones, Hopalong Cassidy, etc. — a main feature, mainly a detective story — Charlie Chan, Bulldog Diamond, Dead End Kids, etc., and a "continued piece" or serial which ran for several weeks with the hero(es) being in imminent danger at the conclusion of each installment. My two favorite "continued pieces" were "Hawk of the Wilderness" and "Fu Manchu." Fu Manchu had one of my favorite bits of movie dialogue. The hero's name was Parker and Fu Manchu had captured him and had him spread-eagled on a bench. A pendulum with a sharp scythe on the end was swinging back and forth above him coming ever closer. Fu Manchu is trying to get Parker to talk. The installment ends with the scythe about to cut Parker in half and Fu Manchu is saying with a sinister leer, "This is your last chance, Mr. Parker!" Of course it wasn't.

There were four five and dime stores in a row on Washington Street. There was a Woolworth, Kress, Grant's and McClellan's. The Lyric Theater was sandwiched in between the Kress and Grant's so you had to pass two five and dimes no matter from what direction you approached the picture show. It was very difficult to pass these trinkets and sweets bazaars on the way to the picture show when you only had a single dime for show fare. It was equally painful to sit slouched down in your seat inside the theater with kids all around you munching on five and dime candy delights. But if you had an extra nickel or dime or a miracle quarter once in a great while, then the situation was totally different.

All five and dime stores were laid out about the same way. There were usually double doors on both sides of the front entrance. At the front of the store, just as you entered, either on the right or left side, would be the candy counter. The candy counters were separated or partitioned into several separate sections about eighteen or twenty inches wide. Each section contained a different kind of candy. There were big square blocks of milk chocolate, huge wedges of fudge and white divinity, orange slices, chocolate kisses, jaw breakers (which we bought a lot since they lasted longer), marbled candies, etc. The candy was sold by the pound, though God knows I never understood this, since it seemed to me there was no one anywhere rich enough to buy a pound of candy. There was a scale behind the counter that had a silver-colored metal hopper on top. The sales lady would scoop the candy up in a metal scoop with a wooden handle and fill the hopper with the purchased amount. Sometimes she would add a few more pieces after the initial scoop and sometimes she would take a few pieces out. She would then tilt the hopper's lip into a white paper bag and pour the candy inside. I remembered reading a piece of sales philosophy in one of the magazines I sold back then. It told the story of a candy clerk in a five and dime store who seemed to always attract the most customers. Many customers would wait for her even though there were other clerks available to wait on them. The manager of the store finally asked her why the people all wanted her to wait on them and why she sold so much more candy than anyone else. She replied, "Most of the other clerks always pour too much candy into the hopper and have to pour some back. I always pour too little so I have to always add some."

The five and dime stores also sold other marvelous edibles such as popcorn and potato chips, which they made themselves. In the summertime, they also sold an unbelievable ice cream sandwich. They would have an ice cream box at the front of the store and the ice cream was Neapolitan and it was in a large brick. The clerk would slice a nice size wedge from the brick and place it between two backed, waffled cake crackers.

The five and dime had waist high (for grown ups) counters down each side of the store and counters running from left to right from the front to the back of the store. Aisles separated all of the counters. All or most of the counters had a small glass fence around the sides and front and also up and down the counters dividing them into various separate sections.

The counters usually contained sections of one type of item, for example, notions, socks, buttons, etc. I was never interested in but two of them — the candy and toy counters. The toys they sold were mainly tops, yo-yos, rick-racks, cap pistols, jacks, jigsaw puzzles, kites, and so forth.

The stores had wooden floors which were always smooth with a thin polished layer of oil on them. There were several overhead revolving fans and I always remember them as cool in the summer and warm in the winter. I spent a lot of happy hours in five and dime stores in Huntsville.

The railroad station was one block from town and you could reach it from either Church or Jefferson Street. I used to love to hear the train whistles blow late at night as I lay in bed and I would dream of traveling all over the country when I got older. I used to go down to the depot and watch the passenger trains come in. People would get on and off and porters would haul baggage carts up and down the trains loading baggage and other items. The mail truck would be there to load the mail. Conductors stood on the platforms, now and then looking at their watches. Finally they would pick up the little iron platform step that they always had at the foot of the steps on and off the cars. They would call, "All aboard!" The train would move slowly out of the station and if it was near any meal time you could see the people eating in the dining cars. There was absolutely nothing that could ever take the place of the old railway cars for a feeling of adventure, mystery, and romance. I have never stopped loving trains.

I remember a particular tragedy when I was a child, however, that I can still see today. An old colored man was hit and run over by a train and they had carried him to one of the baggage cars on the train station platform. Someone had covered him with a sheet of brown butcher wrapping paper, but it did not completely cover him. I remember three things about the old man: the slow dripping of his blood between the cracks of the baggage cart onto the concrete train platform; his protruding teeth; and a small, crushed box of tidbits in his back overall pocket.

I have so many more memories of those days. I remember Blue Bird ice cream, especially dixie cups with movie stars' (particularly cowboys') pictures on the inside of the cup lids. We used to save them and trade with each other like kids did with bubblegum cards. I remember that we made most of the things we played with. Race cars (using old wagon wheels and apple crates), scooters (two pieces of two-by-four and one rollerskate), rubber guns (piece of wood and clothes pin), flips (forked tree limb, tongue from old shoe and two strips of rubber from an inner tube), and many more.

I remember the radio programs. Did I love the radio. Sunday night was really fantastic. I still remember one program and I can hear the announcer now saying, "This is Thomas L. Thomas with the Manhattan Merry-Go-Round!" What images you could create on your own with radio!

I remember Christmas time and what a transformation would take place downtown. Firecracker stands would appear on several corners. Windows would be filled with Christmas decorations, and the stores would stay open late for two weeks prior to Christmas.

It's all gone now, except in my memories.

ELLEN SULLIVAN

Shannon, Alabama

I moved to Alabama in 1974 as a child bride. I never thought I would live in Alabama. From the comfortable perspectives of Minnesota, Connecticut, and Vermont I had watched the terrifying footage of crosses burning; children being kept out of schools; citizens flattened by firehoses. I wasn't so narrow-minded as to think that Alabama didn't have its good points. Most places do. But I never had it picked out in my mind as a place to aim for, like San Francisco or Athens or Popocatapetl.

I only came to Alabama because my husband-to-be wanted to go to Birmingham, and I paid no attention back then to what I wanted. I was still a child.

We came into town in mid-August with our possessions piled in a pick-up truck, covered with an old hooked rug, and tied up in a rope. I remember sailing like a barge on the loose down 3rd Avenue South into town. There was a red light at an auto transmission place that had, hanging from a pole out front, an old transmission with a pair of dummy legs in blue jeans sticking out of it.

For two weeks we stayed at the St. Francis Motor Lodge on Highway 31 in Homewood. We had a ground floor room all done in blue on the alley by the entrance to the swimming pool. Every night we went through that entrance and skirted the cement poolside patio to the King's Inn restaurant. Every night we told the waitress how we wanted our steak done and what kind of dressing on the salad and whether we'd have butter or sour cream on our baked potatoes.

In the daytime we discovered barbecue. Not barbecued hamburgers or chickens or ribs like they have up north: a piece of meat cooked outdoors with bottled sauce on it; but barbecue the miraculous, life-essential southern style: pork or beef juicy, slow-cooked, sliced or chopped and heaped on a plate with a spicy homemade sauce, fries, and cole slaw. With peach or apple fried pie, dripping with melted butter, for dessert. As we found it at Demetri's restaurant this was an unheard of, unimagined heaven. Cooked up by the black ladies who joked with each other around the pit; served by silent, prim white girls. I marveled and gained weight.

We looked for houses to rent. We wanted to live in the country. Up north we knew lots of writers, artists, teachers, and musicians who lived in the country, where they rose at dawn and did their creative work as the mist lifted from the meadows, then went out and hewed down trees and chopped them up, celebrating with lots of good food and wine at night. It looked like a pretty good life, the country life.

Remember this was 1974. We'd just finished getting back to our roots. We both had long hair and I suppose people saw us as hippies. Two young waifs, refugees from the northern megalopolis.

The first place we looked at in the Birmingham area was way out in the country, I have no idea where. It was a shotgun shack, literally. Up on cinder blocks, tarpaper siding, shotgun layout; all the windows on one side of the house were even shot out. The people next door were obese and mean-looking down to the last man, woman, and child. They stared at us with raisinette eyes. I wanted my mother.

We looked at another place on Columbiana Road in Homewood, near the intersection with Oxmoor, where the Palisades shopping plaza is now. The landlady lived next door in a blood red ranch house. She was in her 50s and had a big nest of teased blond hair. She invited us in and asked us what church we belonged to. Our answers, Episcopal and Catholic, did not seem to be what she wanted to hear. Although, looking back, I realize that I did not then know how to have a neighborly conversation with someone, and was expecting to be judged.

We finally called a real estate agent.

Mr. Markham, as I'll call him, picked us up in his brougham and took us Over the Mountain. This was the first time I'd heard that phrase. I learned from Mr. Markham that, in Birmingham, that's where "people like us" would want to live. He winked when he told us.

The house he showed us was west of suburban Homewood, in the small unincorporated town of Shannon. In the country, to be exact, between Homewood and Bessemer. It was right on the main road between the two cities, set back on two sloping wooded acres that fronted a vast pine forest owned, according to Mr. Markham, by something called T.C.I.

The land was lovely. The house was vacant and crude; it had a tin roof, no insulation, a small falling down barn in back, a lopsided garage. I was feverish that day with a sunburn contracted from an innocent Yankee's over-exposure to the Alabama sun. If my young husband-to-be wanted the house — which was for sale, not rent — he could have it. Anything. I just wanted to go back to the motel and lie down.

Mr. Markham cinched the deal by assuring us he could fix us up with two mortgages and would co-sign at the bank for a note, which would create the downpayment we did not have.

Next thing we knew we were in his office in Hoover signing papers in front of the air conditioner, and he was showing us the letters from young couples and old ladies thanking him for making their mobile homes a reality. We had just sold our souls to two mortgage companies and a bank but we didn't know it yet. We went back to the St. Francis Motor Lodge and told them how we wanted our celebratory filet mignons cooked.

So we moved into the house at 1675 Shannon Road. The first thing that happened after that was the neighbors came over. First, Mr. and Mrs. Gettys, the retired couple who lived next door, paid their respects. They brought half of a pound cake on a paper plate covered with foil. Mr. Gettys walked with a heavy favor to one side, like a gyroscope out of balance. She was petite, with her gray hair in a French twist, and one of those plain country faces that are beautiful in the expression the years have stamped upon it: sweetly smiling, even sparkling; a face full of hope.

The Gettyses told us about the Cowarts and "Miz" Grubb, the two respective former owners. They said they themselves had moved to Shannon seven years ago from their 30-year home in

Birmingham's West End, where "the niggers were taking over."
They said this without hostility, just as a statement of fact as they saw
it, which puzzled me. As if they had stated that the sky was clearing
or clouding up. Lots of the neighbors in Shannon had moved here
from West End, they said.

The Gettyses lived with their german shepherd Duke just down
the hill from us, behind our tumbledown barn. The Cowarts had
had goats in here, they told us. "And all that land back 'ere is T.C.I.
land," old J. D. Gettys said, waving his arm to encompass the better
part of Shades Valley. He looked surprised when I asked what T.C.I.
was. "Why, Tennessee Coal and Iron Company," he said.

Across the street lived Louis and his family. I never did figure out
what Louis did for a living. He was home most of the time, building
spotless reassemblages of vintage cars. He came up with his son in
one of them, a blue Ford coupe, and pointed out that we had two
of the best fig trees in the county. We didn't know this, although the
trees were laden with fruit. I'd never seen a fig tree or a fresh fig,
and thought they only grew in places like Tahiti. Louis and his son
went away with a bag full of the fruit, and left us with some peanut
butter cookies Louis' wife had baked.

We were living the country life. We rototilled the entire back
yard and planted a winter garden, a spring garden, a summer
garden. We planted everything we could think of: peanuts, brussels
sprouts, kohlrabi. We didn't know what to plant or how to do it.
We'd never seen red clay and were mystified by ground the color
of rust.

The Gettyses gave us okra and mustard and turnip seeds. What
they gave us grew. Old Mr. Gettys helped. He swore by planting at
the full moon. That and chicken manure. He had a garden as big
as half a football field to prove it.

I started buying my groceries at the Jones Gro. No. 2 in Shannon, a postage stamp of a store run by Wayne Jones, a red-haired
man with a withered arm who told us whatever we did, not to go to
Mississippi. I discovered southern fried vegetables, okra and fried
corn and fried green tomatoes. I learned to talk about the weather.
I began to accept, without paranoia, the greetings of strangers. I
watched with interest as Mr. Gettys, who claimed his dog "just
naturally hated niggers," stood conversing for minutes on end with

our postman, who was black. I was learning that in Alabama, you had your politics, you had your prejudices, you had your traditions; and then you had your daily life. The twain did not necessarily meet.

I also learned the definition of a good neighbor, as told to me by Mrs. Gettys: it's "someone who never bothers you, but is always there when you need them."

Mrs. Gettys was the first person I'd ever seen in my life who put up two Christmas trees at Christmas: the family tree, a green artificial one with colored balls, colored lights, and tinsel, in the family room; and the dressy tree, a white artificial one with pink balls, white icicles, and white flashing lights, in the picture window in the living room.

For our first Christmas in Shannon, the Gettyses gave us a Lane cake and a card telling us we were the best neighbors they'd ever had.

I learned to say "hey" to people and to use the pronoun "y'all." I got two cats. They learned to follow me on long walks into the T.C.I woods, a place where I found a peace of mind and balm for the soul that I'd never really known. These became my woods.

There was an intricate network of paths cross-secting the muffled, dusky-smelling pine-needled floor of my woods. You could walk for miles under the cathedral of the trees, the sun filtering in pale bars from high up in the aromatic ceiling, spackling the earth with light. Honeysuckle and wild muscadine laced themselves around the trunks; there were jewel-like wild iris and dog's tooth violets; rabbit-eye blueberries and a king's ransom in blackberries; and on a hill under the power lines, a gift of grace: a field of wild azalea, their delicate open-lipped flowers porcelain pink or orange as tongues.

Often I took Duke the dog with me on my excursions. There was a quiet joy in his snufflings, his barks of discovery that flushed out rabbits or garden snakes. One time he found a hole that had no bottom; a drilled-out circle maybe five inches in diameter down which I dropped a stone. Duke kept his wet black nose to the hole, ears thrust forward, and I leaned into him as we waited for the stone to drop. But we never heard a landing sound. Just a walla, walla, walla, as it rattled down and down. Then nothing. Duke looked up at me, ears quizzical. And I was happy.

It didn't matter that we were worse than broke, that I couldn't even afford to buy a paperback book. It didn't even matter that our house was shabby, with its leaky roof, mismatched walls, missing closet doors, and a floor full of tacks where I'd pulled up the drab living room carpet in the hope of having the handsome hardwood floors I'd seen in magazines.

I couldn't know then that my marriage would collapse. That T.C.I. would clear cut my beloved forest. That the Pig Trail BBQ down on Highway 150 would turn into the fabulous Galleria, mall of the century. That I would eventually move, alone, to what Mr. Markham would have considered the wrong side of the mountain.

I was at peace in Shannon, Alabama. Life was uncomplicated and whole. It wasn't the happiness I'd once imagined for myself, say, as a screenwriter living on the banks of a Cascade mountain lake, or a journalist shipping out on a freighter for Madagascar. It was real.

RANDALL WILLIAMS

❧ ❧ ❧

LaFayette, Alabama

A bout the time I turned 16, my folks began to wonder why I didn't stay home any more. I always had an excuse for them, but what I didn't say was that I had found my freedom and I was getting out.

I went through four years of high school in semirural Alabama and became active in clubs and sports; I made a lot of friends and became a regular guy, if you know what I mean. But one thing was irregular about me: I managed those four years without ever having a friend visit at my house.

I was ashamed of where I lived. I had been ashamed for as long as I had been conscious of class.

We had a big family. There were several of us sleeping in one room, but that's not so bad if you get along, and we always did. As you get older, though, it gets worse.

Being poor is a humiliating experience for a young person trying hard to be accepted. Even now — several years removed — it is hard to talk about. And I resent the weakness of these words to make you feel what it was really like.

We lived in a lot of old houses. We moved a lot because we were always looking for something just a little better than what we had. You have to understand that my folks worked harder than most people. My mother was always at home, but for her that was a full-time job — and no fun, either. My father worked his head off from the time I can remember in construction and shops. It was hard, physical work.

I tell you this to show that we weren't shiftless. No matter how much money Daddy made, we never made much progress up the social ladder. I got out thanks to a college scholarship and because I was a little more articulate than the average.

I have seen my Daddy wrap copper wire through the soles of his boots to keep them together in the wintertime. He couldn't buy new boots because he had used the money for food and shoes for us. We lived like hell, but we went to school well-clothed and with a full stomach.

It really is hell to live in a house that was in bad shape 10 years before you moved in. And a big family puts a lot of wear and tear on a new house, too, so you can imagine how one goes downhill if it is teetering when you move in. But we lived in houses that were sweltering in summer and freezing in winter. I woke up every morning for a year and a half with plaster on my face where it had fallen out of the ceiling during the night.

This wasn't during the Depression, this was in the late '60s and early '70s.

When we boys got old enough to learn trades in school, we would try to fix up the old houses we lived in. But have you ever tried to paint a wall that crumbled when the roller went across it? And bright paint emphasized the holes in the wall. You end up more frustrated than when you began, especially when you know that at best you might come up with only enough money to improve one of the six rooms in the house. And we might move out soon after, anyway.

The same goes for keeping a house like that clean. If you have a house full of kids and the house is deteriorating, you'll never keep it clean. Daddy used to yell at Mama about that, but she couldn't do anything. I think Daddy knew it inside, but he had to have an outlet for his rage somewhere, and at least yelling isn't as bad as hitting, which they never did to each other.

But you have a kitchen which has no counter space and no hot water, and you will have dirty dishes stacked up. That sounds like an excuse, but try it. You'll go mad from the sheer sense of futility. It's the same thing in a house with no closets. You can't keep clothes clean and rooms in order if they have to be stacked up with things.

Living in a bad house is generally worse on girls. For one thing, they traditionally help their mother with the housework. We boys could get outside and work in the field or cut wood or even play ball and forget about living conditions. The sky was still pretty.

But the girls got the pressure and as they got older it became worse. Would they accept dates knowing they had to "receive" the young man in a dirty hallway with broken windows, peeling wallpaper and a cracked ceiling? You have to live it to understand it, but it creases a shame which drives the soul of a young person inward.

I'm thankful none of us ever blamed our parents for this, because it could have crippled our relationships. As it worked out, only the relationship between our parents was damaged. And I think the harshness which they expressed to each other was just an outlet to get rid of their anger at the trap their lives were in. It ruined their marriage because they had no one to yell at but each other. I knew other families where the kids got the abuse, but we were too much loved for that.

Once I was about 16 and Mama and Daddy had a particularly violent argument about the washing machine, which had broken down. Daddy was on the back porch — that's where the only water faucet was — trying to fix it and Mama had a washtub out there washing school clothes for the next day and they were screaming at each other.

Later that night everyone was in bed and I heard Daddy get up from the couch where he was reading. I looked out from my bed across the hall into their room. He was standing right over Mama and she was already asleep. He pulled the blanket up and tucked it around her shoulders and just stood there and tears were dropping off his cheeks and I thought I could faintly hear them splashing against the linoleum rug.

Now they're divorced.

I had courses in college where housing was discussed, but the sociologists never put enough emphasis on the impact that living in substandard housing has on a person's psyche. Especially children's. Small children have a hard time understanding poverty. They want the same things children from more affluent families have. They want the same things they see advertised on television, and they don't understand why they can't have them.

Other children can be incredibly cruel. I was in elementary school in Georgia — and this is interesting because it is the only thing I remember about that particular school — when I was about eight or nine.

After Christmas vacation had ended, my teacher made each student describe all his or her Christmas presents. I became more and more uncomfortable as the privilege passed around the room toward me. Other children were reciting the names of the dolls they had been given, the kinds of bicycles and the grandeur of their games and toys. Some had lists which seemed to go on and on for hours.

It took me only a few seconds to tell the class that for Christmas I had gotten a belt and a pair of gloves. And then I was laughed at — because I cried — by a roomful of children and a teacher. I never forgave them, and that night I made my mother cry when I told her about it.

In retrospect, I am grateful for that moment, but I remember wanting to die at the time.

NED McDAVID

❧ ❧ ❧

Birmingham, Alabama

I was born in St. Vincent's Hospital in 1927. My mother was
from Troy and my father was from Birmingham. My maternal
grandmother was an adventuress and writer. She had been
with her husband to South America and she wrote stories about it.
I think at least one was published. She also went to Hollywood to try
to be a screenwriter.

My father's family, the McDavids, were prominent in Birmingham. The family business was R.P. McDavid & Sons, the RCA
representative.

My father was Edward and he had three brothers. One was R.P.
II (Duke), and another was Joe (Broadway), who was about five feet
two inches tall and weighed 300 pounds. He was in Walter Winchell's
column one time when he visited New York and forever after he was
"Broadway Joe." Another brother was Charles (Chick), and his
sisters were Virginia and Martha.

Uncle Duke and his sister Virginia had conflicting life styles, and
for a little kid it was fascinating to visit both households. Generally
we went to Aunt Virginia's for Sunday dinner, and I always wore a
coat and tie at five or six. We were poor, living in Forest Park, and
Aunt Virginia was affluent with a house on Country Club Road and
two or three servants. Lewis was the butler and chauffeur and he
wore a black silk suit when he served Sunday dinner. When he
drove he wore a tall black silk hat. My father was bad to drink, so
alcohol was not present at the home of family members. I don't
recall ever seeing any of them drink at home or entertain with
cocktail parties; however, they drank at the Club. All of the McDavid
men "disappeared" occasionally to the Gulf Coast to drink and my

father was the worst. Once every six weeks he disappeared. When this happened, my mother would take me to the Thomas Jefferson Hotel and check in. I loved to do this because I could go to the movies all day for a dime. The movies were the Ritz, the Alabama, the Pantages, the Strand and the Galax. When my father appeared again we would go back home. He worked at the family business, but Lord how he hated being a salesman and tradesman.

John Guyton, a black man, was much devoted to all the McDavids. If one disappeared he would show up with money, a car or whatever was missing. He really worked for Uncle Broad (Joe), who was a bachelor and could get away with his drinking. When my daddy would leave, John Guyton would appear with what he called "Time" (money). He called me "Mr. Zilch," and he would say, "Mr. Zilch, you got some time?" "No, Mr. Guyton," I would reply. "I ain't got no time." "Well, Mr. Zilch, I'll slip you some time," he would say and chuckle. John Guyton filched money from my relatives to bring money to my mother.

I loved to go to town on Saturday. The bus cost seven cents, so it was fourteen cents to and from town. The Mickey Mouse Club and movie cost twenty cents and a hot dog was five cents. Also, I would go to Kress and buy two toy soldiers for five cents apiece. I stayed all day in town for less than a dollar.

I would go to Aunt Minnie V.'s and Uncle Duke's house, and this was like going to the house of "You can't take it with you." Going to Aunt Virginia's house was like going to Myrna Loy and William Powell's place on Park Avenue.

Aunt Minnie V. stayed in bed all day reading mystery novels. Her children were Robert III, Henry, Leroy, and Martha. Only Martha went to school. They were all sickly and had to sleep until noon. My father called Henry "Taylor" because he was handome like the movie actor, Robert Taylor. Eating over there was great fun for it was catch as catch can. We might have sandwiches for dinner or anything we wanted. In those days butter came with yellow color packages and we would get back in the kitchen with Carrie and color batches of butter.

My mother and Aunt Minnie V. were big buddies. She would take me with her to visit Aunt Minnie in her bedroom. On the bed there was always a wooden case of cokes and there were three or four big old dogs hanging around.

I had a miserable childhood really. I was asthmatic and Birmingham was damp, grey, and polluted. We didn't have any money and we moved all the time. I hated Lakeview School; there was a lot of keeping up with the Joneses. I was smart in school, but I was sickly.

One of the high points I recall was when they took me to Montgomery to an Auburn-Florida football game when I was about nine. That was the first time I saw drinking at home.

After the war, or during it, several of the ones who didn't go to school like Robert II, Leroy, and Henry, went to the University of Alabama at times. They went one or two years to "Jelly Bean," my father said. Martha was the only McDavid to graduate from college after grandfather, and then I did.

When I was twelve my mother divorced my father. Grandmother came up in a new car she bought from selling property, and we moved to Miami. My Aunt Emaline had lost her husband and was afraid to live alone with her two children. We moved in with her and stayed about two years. I burned up a lot next door trying to smoke a cigarette.

In the meantime, my father had moved to Palm Beach. I went on the bus to visit him for a few days; that was a sad time. He bought me a rod and reel and I fished Saturday. That night he left. A young girlfried of his came and took me to dinner. We had a nice time and she came home awhile with me. I read a book until late waiting for my daddy, but he never came. The next morning she came with me to the bus. He wrote and apologized, but I was so embarrassed to come home early. I didn't want anyone to know I had divorced parents anyway, but everyone must have known because I came home early.

My mother soon remarried and we moved to Bonifay, Florida, where her husband was in the family lumber business. My father finally remarried again, too. He married an old maid with a sister. The two women took care of him the rest of his life.

JANIE L. SHORES

🐦 🐦 🐦

Georgiana, Alabama

The first job I had was picking strawberries. My mother and sister and I joined many others, old and young, black and white, in the fields early in the morning. Someone brought lunch on a pickup truck. I don't remember what we ate but I remember drinking Grapettes. This must have been in the late '30s. My father John, mother Willie, sister Verla and I lived about three miles south of Georgiana, in Butler County. I was maybe six years old.

After Pearl Harbor we moved to Baldwin County, to Loxely. My father got a job in Mobile.

Verla and I shortly got our next job. She was nine by then, and I would have been eleven. We picked up potatoes for a nickel a basket. I remember being embarrassed because my fair and freckle-prone skin compelled me to wear long sleeves and a hat.

The potato harvest in Baldwin County began in April. School started early in August and ended early to accommodate the harvest season.

Before the first year was over I got a promotion from a mere picker to bookkeeper. My job was to keep track of the number of baskets which picker picked up. Each picker kept a count by putting a tiny potato in his or her pocket each time a basket was filled. These were turned over to me at the end of each row. It was up to me to keep the pickers honest by occasionally checking to see that their baskets equaled the tiny potatoes.

While Verla and I earned as much as $3 a day — 60 baskets, sometimes more — my mother Willie was earning $30 to $50 a week as a waitress and then as a telephone operator.

About that time, my father John was sent by the Navy for basic training to Great Lakes, Michigan. He came home only once before "shipping out" to the Pacific, where he spent the duration of the war.

Both Verla and I had found jobs on the shed by my fifteenth summer. The shed was the place where the potatoes were brought by truck to be washed and graded, by size. The little ones would fall through holes in the tracks and be carried on different belts. The little ones were "Bs." Women worked on each side of the tracks picking out rotten or damaged potatoes. The remaining ones went into sacks which were sewn up, usually by men, and were carted into railroad cars. We earned 40 cents an hour.

I eventually became a sewer, one of the few women who did. I was in the shed when the atomic bomb was dropped on Hiroshima. We were shipping cucumbers. I was there when the war ended. I was sitting on the front porch when President Roosevelt died, so the shed must not have opened up yet that year. President Roosevelt had been elected the year I was born.

With the war over, my father came home and went back to work at the shipyards, and things were not much different. He worked the second shift, which I think was 4 p.m. to midnight. I was frequently outside when he came home, trying to get over a siege of nausea, which I had all my life. It would wake me up in the middle of the night. They said I had a nervous stomach. Daddy would say, "Sick again, Janie Lee?" and I would answer "Yes sir." He would go on in and go to bed.

By this time Verla and I had both gotten jobs as waitresses in the summer. I didn't like it much and wasn't very good at it, but it was better than the shed. Willie was still working at the telephone office. Verla and I used to go there after school and spot airplanes. There was a little chart with pictures of all kinds of airplanes, and you were supposed to circle the kind you saw and put the date by it. I remember seeing a P-38. It had two fuselages. I don't know who picked up the charts or where they came from. I don't know what purpose they served, but it was considered patriotic to do it.

My brother Larry was born in September of 1948. I was 16, Verla was 14, Willie was 32, and John was 33. We all adored him. Verla and I left school at noon to keep him, because John had to leave for work before school got out, and Willie didn't get home until after five. I don't think Verla and I ever had a babysitter, and I don't believe Larry did either.

Shortly before my graduation from Robertsdale High School in April of 1950, I got a job in an office! In a law office! I had looked all spring. Every Saturday I would get the greyhound bus in front of our house and go to Mobile. I would answer help wanted ads in the paper. I was turned down by most of them because I didn't have any experience.

I finally went on to an employment agency, reluctantly, because they charged a fee. I regret that I have forgotten her name, but a beautiful dark-haired woman, beautifully dressed, said she might be able to get me an interview with a lawyer named Vincent Kilborn, who represented the Bishop.

It was a Saturday afternoon and he answered the telephone himself. I went to his office, at 307 First National Bank Building, telephone 2-26365 (later changed to Hemlock 2-2635). I shall never forget either. I took dictation all afternoon and caught the greyhound home. I went to work full-time the following Monday. My salary was $100 per month.

The hours were 8 til 4:30, but after a few weeks I got permission to change mine to 7:30 til 5, so I could get the 5:30 bus home. The new hours were fine with Mr. Kilborn because he always got to the office by seven anyway.

I stayed with him for four years and they were the most significant years of my life. College had never been mentioned at home, probably because it was a subject none of us knew anything about. Verla and I would talk about getting jobs, but I don't remember ever talking about careers with John and Willie. College wasn't promoted much in school either. I don't know why. Maybe the teachers knew most of us couldn't afford to go anyway and so just didn't talk about it. Anyway, Vince Kilborn was the first adult who encouraged me to go, and not just to college, but to law school. He changed my life.

I took my first college course in 1954, and was graduated from law school in 1959.

Before I was elected to the State Supreme Court, Vince died. It is the only thing I'll never forgive him for.

BETTYE K. WRAY

Birmingham, Alabama

My father was Roy Templin, a native of Columbiana, Alabama. He was one of four children born to Maudie Richard and L. M. Templin, members of early families settling in that area. My father passed the Alabama Bar, and was a clerk in the old Columbiana Courthouse in the earlier working days. His parents owned a large farm three miles outside Columbiana in the direction of the Old Kingdom area. L.M. Templin also "worked in town" at the cotton gin. In the late 1940s the homeplace was sold and a new home was purchased near Main Street. My father's only sister was married to the last blacksmith in Columbiana.

My mother was Onzelle Faust, a native of the Camp Branch-Saginaw area of Shelby County. She was one of six children born to Susan Elizabeth Wilder and Lerner Brooks Faust (two died in infancy). Her parents owned a large farm. Lerner Brooks Faust was a farmer, teacher, and preacher. Susan Elizabeth Wilder was the granddaughter of Hosea Holcomb, the founder of several churches in or near the Birmingham area, and one of the early pioneers in the Southern Baptist Convention. It was said many times that my mother's father made the best sugarcane syrup in Shelby County, and that her mother made the best butter. In the late 1940s my mother's parents sold their homeplace and moved to Birmingham where they lived until their deaths, both living until they were in their 90s.

Where do memories begin? I was born in December 1926 but the first impression of my life began in October 1930, just prior to my fourth birthday.

My parents, a younger brother, and myself lived in the Ensley area of Birmingham. At that time my father was a sales representative for Roberts & Son and traveled outside the city of Birmingham; usually he was away one week at a time. In that particular October and on a Monday morning, he kissed my mother and us children good-bye, saying that he would return on the following Friday and then take us to the "Fair" on Saturday. He was killed in an automobile accident near Gadsden, Alabama, on Friday.

My father was the first person I had seen in a coffin. I remember this vividly. The custom in that area was to bring a deceased person to their home after being at the undertaking parlor, before they were laid to rest in the cemetery. My father was in the parlor-room. I still remember the relatives and many other people in that room. I recall that during that time the paperboy threw an afternoon paper and I ran onto the porch to pick it up. I was wearing an ecru-colored pongee dress with smocking around the top. I had a "Buster Brown" haircut.

My father was 30 years old when he left us and my mother was 27. After his death my mother moved us into a house in the Fairview section of Birmingham. She took a course at Massey Business College, and in a short time went to work for the old Birmingham Electric Company. The Birmingham Electric Company not only serviced the city with electricity, but also operated the streetcar service. There were no city buses and not everyone owned an automobile. Just about everyone rode the streetcars. Mother remained with the "Electric Company" (which later became part of the Alabama Power Company) for 37 years and then retired. She received a gold watch for service, which I wear proudly today.

I have many memories of Fairview days. We lived across the street from Fairview Grammar School and this is where I began my school days. At the corner, and also across the street from our house, was Mr. Spark's store. I thought this a delightful place because one could purchase cookies and penny candy.

My idol in those days was Mildred (Mickey) Oxford, who resided several blocks from my home. She was a terrific tap dancer and later was in the Miss Alabama Pageant. I thought her brother Jerry (Buddy) Oxford, was very special, too. He wore clean white shirts with a tie to school daily, and knickers that never had holes at the knees. Playing marbles was a favorite pastime for boys, and bending down to play the game caused most to get holes in their knicker knees. Not Jerry's!

The fairgrounds were located near our home in Fairview. It was not called the Alabama State Fairgrounds, it was called Fair Park. The statue of Vulcan stood there just inside the gate for a number of years, before he was moved atop Red Mountain with the beautiful flowers and goldfish ponds at his feet. He was not called Vulcan, he was called "The Iron Man." I remember one of his arms had been placed on the statue incorrectly and had to be changed. When he was at Fair Park there was a base around the statue that afforded a place to sit, and I remember many times I sat there looking up at him.

I recall Shirley Temple movies at the "picture show," and dolls that resembled her and bore her name. Little girls had books of paper dolls that cost 10 cents each that came from the five and dime stores. In those days the five and dime stores were really places selling "treasures" that could be purchased for those prices.

As early as Fairview days I would attend the Mickey Mouse Club on Saturdays at the Alabama Theatre. It would seem that every little girl and boy was taking tap dancing lessons, and I was no different. I really had great aspirations of being a singer, but took tap dancing lessons because everyone else was doing it. Later, I did appear on the stage during a few Mickey Mouse programs and sang on WSGN radio. I especially recall one song I liked to sing, "Ah, Sweet Mystery of Life." One must mention that those were also the days of Jeanette McDonald and Nelson Eddy. I wanted to be a classical or opera singer.

When I was nine years old, my mother bought a home in West End on St. Charles Avenue, a few blocks from the Arlington antebellum home. At that time Mr. and Mrs. Montgomery (she had been a Munger) owned the home. They were prominent members of Walker Memorial Methodist Church, where my family also attended and were members. I sang in the choir, as did Mrs. Montgomery, who had a lovely voice. Many Christmases, church members would go around the area singing Christmas carols, and Arlington was one of our stops. We would be invited into the mansion, and given enormous California oranges. The interior of Arlington was always beautiful. I remember the deep, deep rugs throughout, and especially in the large room that held the gigantic Christmas tree and the piano. I can still recall seeing Mr. Montgomery sitting in his study reading. The little guest house, at the rear of the mansion that is used today for meetings and other social functions, was a place where the children could meet and play games such as table ping-pong, checkers, and dominoes.

Growing up on St. Charles Avenue was a time of wonderful memories. Mother never remarried; she continued to work. (She lived in this house 45 years.) She always had time for my brother and me. We were loved and had a very happy, secure childhood.

The late 1930s and 1940s were the days of The Big Bands (Tommy Dorsey and Glenn Miller). Oliver Naylor, Sr., who was a well-known orchestra leader in Birmingham at that time, was one of our neighbors. Our neighborhood was made up of so many children, and Oliver Naylor, Jr. was one of our friends. Everyone went to Elyton Grammar School. There is so much to remember about that school, especially Miss Sara Asbell, my literature teacher. It was because of this lady and her classes that I first realized I was interested in poetry and writing.

I recall wearing "evening dresses" at any special occasion, such as children's birthday parties, ballroom dancing parties for dancing students, and for performances on the Mickey Mouse Club stage. Wearing an evening dress meant a time of excitement. They were made of velvet or taffeta . . . and then there were the lovely net ones over taffeta that rustled and rustled. To go with the dress, there was always a large ribbon worn in the hair. Velvet took precedence, but ribbons were also made of grosgrain or taffeta. I would hold my hands out "ever so big" and mother would make the ribbons around them and tie securely. And, oh the joy of owning a pair of golden evening slippers!

For many years my mother worked six days a week at the Electric Company, later only half-days on Saturdays. I have delightful memories of many of those Saturdays, when I would meet her at noon under the clock outside Loveman's Department Store. We would have lunch at the luncheonette on the balcony inside the store, or we would go up to 20th Street and eat at the Corner Soda. It was located across the street from the Frank Nelson Building and earlier had been called the Paramount Grill. One of the earlier managers there would talk to us and from time to time give us pieces of delicious walnut candies covered with white crunchy-type icing. Always included in the shopping treats would be a visit to Newberry's where one could browse through tables of materials for dresses. We would buy material by the yard and always located good bargains on the remnant table. If a special material was needed it could almost always be found at Burger-Phillips. Mother was also an expert seamstress and made many of our clothes.

Our home was heated by the arcola coal heating system. I believe that almost everyone had a coal pile in their backyard. We did, and I recall making some of my most "glamorous" photographs standing beside it. The coal pile was secondary to the coal being delivered and put in an outside storage shed or house. One would bring coal inside in a skuttle to leave beside the arcola. Because of convenience, I suppose the coal pile was necessary.

I remember playing in the rain on summer days in old cotton dresses. We would pretend we were at the swimming pool. At times we did go to the swimming pool, and Cascade Plunge was a favorite. We would roll over and over in the cool grass looking for four-leaf clovers and make necklaces and bracelets out of clover blossoms. We loved dandelions, too, although our yard held sweetpeas, larkspur, snapdragons, and tuberoses. Mother had a special side yard garden where lovely radiant roses seemed to be always in bloom.

We would sit on the front porch and swing in the big swing. One summer evening I fondly recall we were swinging and singing "Deep Purple" and "Blue Moon" and some Stephen Foster favorites, too.

There was a cozy fireplace in the living room. I was sitting on the sofa in front of the fireplace when a neighbor came in to tell us Pearl Harbor had been bombed on December 7, 1941.

Just prior to World War II, the 27th Division for Ft. McClellan came through Birmingham going to Arkansas for maneuvers. They traveled in the army trucks along Lomb Boulevard (Avenue), which was not completely paved at that time, and which was located near my home. Later I met one of the soldiers in that division and we were married. He transferred into the Rangers and was one of the American servicemen who landed on the beaches of Normandy on D-Day. He was a recipient of two Bronze Stars and three Purple Hearts. After he returned from combat we lived in New York and had a happy life together until 1963 when he died of a heart attack. I returned to Birmingham with my two daughters. Mother was still living in the house on St. Charles Avenue. I believe it was Truman Capote who said if you ever live in Alabama, you will one day return, usually remaining. In my case it was true.

WAYNE GREENHAW

Colbert County, Alabama

My Granddaddy, called Uncle Bub Able by his friends, was a union man. He had cut his teeth in the labor union building Wilson Dam for the Tennessee Valley Authority. He was a carpenter then, hammering and sawing to build the cofferdams.

When I was a little boy growing up in his household, because my Daddy was overseas in the Army and my Mama was working in a military aircraft plant, the most prominently displayed items were a Franklin Delano Roosevelt clock and a picture of a birthday-cake-decorated float. Sometimes I'd stare for a long while at the two prizes.

Once on a sweltering north Alabama night in mid-August he said, "Son, that's the finest clock in the whole wide world." On the face were the tin figures of a fife player and two drummers. The hand of one drummer ticktocked loudly with every second's beat. The face was a circle forming the middle of a ship's helm next to which stood President Roosevelt, shoulders wide, head aloof, and eyes focused on the future. Across the base of the clock was the inscription: FDR: THE MAN OF THE HOUR.

My Granddaddy was crippled when I knew him. He hobbled about on a walking cane, injured when he fell more than 200 feet down an embankment while constructing Wheeler Dam for the T.V.A.

He was long since retired from the carpenter trade, but he always liked to remember. "I'll never forget that night when I bought that clock. Me and your Nanny and your Mama were living in a tent in Sheffield. It was hard times back then. It was the middle of the Depression. I had worked every job I could get, but nothing came steady. We moved in that tent all over Alabama, Mississippi, and part of Tennessee. Your Nanny and your Mama never complained. Every time I'd get a new job, they'd pick up and we'd move.

"When I went to work for T.V.A. I signed on with the union. I had worked as a carpenter off and on for five years or better. I had all the experience I needed. I knew what to do once an engineer told me what the plans were. When I signed with the union and attended the first meeting and heard those fellows talk about brotherhood and working regular and putting meat on the table along with blackeyed peas and turnip greens, I felt kind of funny — good all over.

"I had heard a lot about unions. I never did want to join though. I'd gone to a Ku Klux Klan meeting back in Tuscaloosa in the '20s. People compared the union with the Ku Klux Klan back then. I went to just one meeting. When I got there I saw why they wore hoods over their faces.

"They were some of the sorriest, no-account people in the community. Several I knew owed on their bills and never intended to pay, and they were sitting there cursing poor colored people. It made me sick. I left and never went back.

"But the union meeting was something else. It was kind of like a church meeting almost. It made me feel real good. I told Emma, your grandmother, that night that it was the best thing I'd ever done. She told me that was fine. I told her everybody was looking toward tomorrow instead of worrying about today. They could see something better coming in front of us. She said she could see why I felt the way I did. She hugged me and kissed me. She wanted to believe just as much as I did.

"That Friday when I got paid the biggest amount of money I had ever got for a week's work, I stopped off with some of the other labor union people I worked with, toasted the President of the United States with a drink of straight whiskey, and started home.

"When I got to a drugstore I saw that clock in the window. Franklin Delano Roosevelt was standing there." His voice almost cracked. "I don't think I even looked to see how much the price was. I went inside and bought it. I carried it home and put it next to my chair. Emma looked at it and shook her head. Your Mama touched it very softly. I told 'em we'd have to keep that clock forever. It was a sign that everything would be all right."

When he saw me looking at the photograph, he explained that it had been made on a downtown street in Sheffield, Alabama, and that the small figure standing on the back of the float was he himself. It was his first Labor Day celebration as an officer in the carpenter's local. He was very proud of that day.

"We worked hard. We built dams. We were paid good wages for that day. We hoped that our hours would go to develop something good for you and your children," he said, and patted me on the shoulder.

Today, when I look at the clock on the mantel over my fireplace, I remember his words. When I feel sorry for myself because I don't have a Cadillac or a speedboat or some other luxury I don't need anyway, I stare at the motionless clock and think of the suffering and good times that went into it.

Every Labor Day I feel a special happiness when I view the parade of proud union people on their day of rest. Seeing the floats decorated in their many colors, I remember that white float with its red and yellow trim.

It made my Granddaddy happy to look at it and remember when he was an officer in his local. And it makes me happy to picture the glow of his eyes in my mind's eye.

HELEN SHORES LEE

❦ ❦ ❦

Birmingham, Alabama

It was a hot, muggy summer night in 1953. I was sitting with my family on the front porch of our home on Center Street in Birmingham. All was quiet except for the sounds of crickets and a few cars passing every now and then.

Suddenly a car filled with white youths came down the hill, slowed in front of our house, shone a spotlight in our faces and shouted racial obscenities. Then they sped away, only to turn around and pass by again, shining the light at us and calling us names.

My father, always placid and self-contained, told us to ignore them. But I was burning with anger. I wanted to shout back; I argued with my father, but he was insistent. Still I was burning up inside.

As the car sped away, I got up and went into the house. I remember that my father kept an old Colt .45 hidden in his closet. Carefully I removed the gun from its holster and returned to the front porch to wait. Soon the car of white youths came down the hill again, shouting "Niggers go home!"

I took aim but as I prepared to fire, my father hit my arm. The shot was deflected into the air. He snatched the gun from me. Still using a quiet, rational voice, he asked me if I knew that I would go to jail if I hit one of them — possibly, even probably, for life. The impact of what he'd said struck me, and I started to cry. But I was still furious.

"It's not fair," I wept. "We were just minding our own business."

I couldn't understand how it was legal for someone to harass us, but not legal for us to respond.

I was only twelve years old at the time, but that night stands out in my memory as a graphic example of how, in a moment of fear and anger, each of us has the potential to ruin lives.

That night was also the beginning of a series of racial incidents that molded my youth, tested my adulthood, and finally drove me from Birmingham for 13 years. I was angry that night, and looking back, I think I stayed angry for a long time. Anger became part of the fabric of my being.

Nobody ever asked me what it was like to be the daughter of Arthur Shores, Alabama's first black lawyer, the first black to run for the state legislature, and the man behind the headlines of so many southern civil rights cases.

I suppose they never asked because it was generally assumed that the children of Arthur Shores were privileged, stuck-up, over-educated, and "in whitey's pocket." How I hated those labels! When I was growing up it seemed that all my life I had longed to be normal: to be able to give my phone number to my friends, to be able to walk to and from school like all the other kids.

But for much of my youth these things were not possible. Because of my father's involvement in controversial cases, our family's safety was always a concern. Threatening phone calls were part of our lives.

So we were considered "different," my sister Barbara and I. We were not just different from whites; we were different from other blacks, too. We didn't want to be, but that's the way we were perceived.

I remember the first time I realized that there was a barrier between black and white.

I was about seven years old and our family was out for the traditional Sunday drive. Every Sunday after dinner we went for a drive, rain or shine, winter or summer, every Sunday of the year. One Sunday we must have been driving out toward Bessemer, because we went past the Kiddieland at the state fairgrounds. It was lit up like some kind of fairyland; the ferris wheel was going around and the place was swarming with children and their parents. I could smell the cotton candy and hear the music.

I remember begging Dad to take us there. I wanted to go to Kiddieland so badly I could hardly stand it. But my father said no. We couldn't go there now, because only white people could go to Kiddieland. But, he assured us, one day we would be able to go.

I cried and got mad and pouted and said that I wished I was white. I remember to this day exactly what my father said: "Never wish to be white, chickadee. Just wish to go."

As I got older, I naturally became more and more aware of segregation and its implications, especially in terms of what I could do or could not do. Certain practices were never questioned, I suppose because they had been around for so long that both white and black saw them as just "the way things were."

It didn't bother me, for example, to eat at a separate lunch counter in the basement of a downtown department store; it seemed "normal" to go around to the back of the streetcar and get on board. It was part of the order of things that the dime store put candy and peanuts in white bags with waxed paper lining for white people, but in a plain brown paper sack for blacks.

Oddly enough, Mama always got a white sack, because she was so light-skinned she was often taken for white. This too, I accepted as a fact of life. I remember when she took me to get my driver's license I sailed right through the test because the people at the courthouse assumed Mama was white, and that I was her black maid! After that it became a family joke; relatives would ask my mother to take them to get their licenses. And she even did it a few times.

But segregation wasn't really funny. More often, it brought out that hot temper of mine, and I would openly rebel. For example, although the separate lunch counter in the department store went unquestioned, the separate water fountains posed a challenge. I remember that white drinking fountain: clean, gleaming white porcelain, with a sign over it that read "Whites Only." And around the corner from it the black drinking fountain: small, old, and dirty.

I was determined that I was going to drink from that white-only fountain. I remember going purposefully over to it and taking great delight in a long slow drink. A white man came up to me, though, and jerked me away, telling me that I knew better than to drink from that fountain. My mother, too, was furious, and told me the same thing. But I was sullen and defiant.

Another time I moved the sign that separated the white and black sections of the streetcar up a few seats, so my mother and I could sit down. I sat, but Mama was upset over what I'd done, and she fearfully remained standing.

I was scolded time and again by my mother for my defiance. It got worse as I came to realize that not only were we different because we were black, we were different because we were the family of Arthur Shores. And there was nothing we could do about it. It was all these feelings that came to a head the hot summer night I tried to shoot at the white youths in the car.

My young life began to look up, however, when I was finally old enough to go to high school.

From the first through the eighth grade, I had attended Lutheran School, a block from where we lived on First Street. Lutheran School had only one classroom and one teacher, Mrs. Longhorn. Mrs. Longhorn taught us all at one time in that room: religion, health, math, English, spelling, and history. There were only three students in my class and about 40 in the whole school.

After I'd finished the seventh grade, Mrs. Longhorn decided that I was ready to go on to high school, and I was delighted. I went to Parker High School, and as a high school student, I was allowed to walk to and from school. I had begun to date by then, and walking to school and home again was critical to the dating process — that was when we did our socializing and our courting.

Much to my dismay, however, walking became out of the question when my father got involved in the integration of the University of Alabama, with the Autherine Lucy case in 1955. Miss Lucy ultimately became the first black student accepted by the University, although she only attended for a few days, primarily due to the uproar her admission caused — an uproar that culminated in George Wallace's famous stand in the schoolhouse door. My father Arthur Shores was her lawyer.

At the time, I didn't exactly appreciate the fact that I had a front row seat to history in the making. All I knew was that now we had to be driven to and from school, because there had been so many threats of kidnapping, and threats on our lives. Security men guarded the house all night, jumping on any stranger who approached. I remember once they pinned a Western Union messenger to the ground before he was identified and allowed to deliver a telegram.

Only a few relatives and very close friends could call on us, and we were forbidden to give out our phone number. I couldn't even give it to my boyfriend. That didn't stop the threatening calls, however, and we had to have our number changed sometimes as often as every three or four days.

I remember I slept with a gun under my pillow and Barbara slept with a baton under hers, and we'd lie awake at night and talk about what we'd do if someone tried to get us.

Looking back, it's easy to see that all the precautions were necessary. But I resented the situation with a passion, mainly because it made most of the kids at school think that we were "stuck-up." Here I was, the girl who refused to give out her phone number; who got delivered to school and picked up from school every day. (Barbara was still in Mrs. Longhorn's class at this time.) All I wanted was to be able to walk home with the other kids, flirt with the boys, and stop for a sandwich at Palmer's barbecue, like everyone else did.

Occasionally, I remember, my boyfriend and I would dodge the man who came to pick me up, by cutting through the projects and back alleys behind the school.

Of course, there were tremedous benefits to growing up under such conditions, but like most young people, I only saw the restrictions that were placed upon me, not the benefits. I wish I could have appreciated, for example, the personalities who would come and go through our house.

During the Lucy case, I remember that Thurgood Marshall, now a justice of the U.S. Supreme Court, and Constance Motley, now a judge in New York, stayed with us. They were both lawyers at that time, and were working with Dad on the Lucy case. They stayed with us as a safety precaution; it would have been much too dangerous for them to have stayed at a motel.

I do remember that I liked Thurgood Marshall a lot; he was friendly and a lot of fun, and always seemed to have time for us children. When I was younger he used to play cowboy with me on the living room floor. During another visit he brought Barbara and me matching cowboy bedspreads, which I think my mother still has somewhere around the house.

But during the Lucy case, my liking for Mr. Marshall was definitely outweighed by the restrictions the case placed upon our lives. My father never seemed bothered by it. He never seemed angry or afraid. He's always been calm, soft-spoken, and philosophical.

My mother, on the other hand, was frightened much of the time, something I never realized until lately. There were guards to take us to school, and guards that followed Dad to work, and guards around the house at night. But during the day, Mama was home alone. She developed a bad case of asthma during this time, and I think it was also during this time that she began to ask my father to leave Birmingham . . . saying that it wasn't worth it to live like this.

But this was where Dad was born and raised; his roots were here, his people, and this was where we'd stay.

I, on the other hand, decided I would leave Alabama at the earliest opportunity.

Dad had always stressed to us that we must get an education; an education was your ticket to freedom. After graduating high school I enrolled at Fisk University in Nashville and began to pursue my goals, determined that I'd never return home. I met my husband Robert, also an Alabama native, during my college years. I participated in the Nashville demonstrations of the '60s that were led by Diana Nash, a classmate of mine. I kept up with what was going on in Birmingham and it only strengthened my conviction to stay away.

Robert and I were married in 1962 and moved to California, where we stayed until 1972. During that time my parents' home was bombed twice; I came back the second time, in 1963, when my mother was injured in the blast. I was furious — burning with that same anger I'd felt on the porch so many years ago. I tried to convince them to leave Alabama; to move to California with us. Mama wanted to, but Dad still refused. He loved Alabama in spite of it all.

Robert and I did end up coming back twice a year, every year, to visit. And eventually, I began to see changes. I have to admit I didn't want to see them, but I did. Things began to change very quickly, in fact. It seemed as if a page in a book had been turned and Birmingham had entered a new chapter.

I was suspicious of the change; I found it hard to believe. People were so cordial . . . the hate and tention seemed to melt away. I began to look for traces of the old ways, to prove to myself that the change wasn't real. But I couldn't find any such evidence.

My mother even reported to me proudly during one visit that she'd taken my children to Kiddieland.

Robert and I decided to move back in 1971. I'm glad my children are growing up in Alabama, near their grandparents, near their history. And I'm proud of what Birmingham and Alabama — and the South — have become. I must say I've come a long way too, from the defiant little girl who wanted to shoot someone from her porch one night in 1953.

JANE L. WEEKS

❧ ❧ ❧

Birmingham, Alabama

The year was 1938, late fall. In a small Catholic hospital in Meridian, Mississippi, a baby was born, a girl. She was the much-awaited first child of Dorothy Louise Middleton Pearson and Delmar Lynn (Shorty to his friends) Pearson, but more important, she was the first grandchild of Hazel Elizabeth Boutwell Middleton (and only incidentally George Douglas Middleton). After four years of trying Dot had finally birthed a baby! I was, of course, the second grandchild of Carrie Porter Pearson and William Thomas Pearson, but the other child was a boy.

My dad and mother were high school sweethearts. She married beneath herself and he married above himself; and this seemed to be the cause of the trouble. He was athletic, lettered in all four major sports, and she played basketball and tennis. Both came from families of railroad men, his from shop workers and hers from middle management. It is my own assessment that he could not live with her and did not want to live without her, and her family's disdain (for want of a better word) made life mighty uncomfortable for him. He began to drink heavily, and it became so bad that many of my early memories are of loud arguments and abusive behavior.

When I was about four years old my mother went to live in the home of my maternal grandmother. It's strange that after all these years I still think of it as her house. My grandfather was a wonderful, seemingly maternal man, wise and honorable, but he only made the big family decisions. A somewhat educated man for his day, my grandfather Middleton had completed two years of college when he married my grandmother over the objections of both families;

she was sixteen and very beautiful. I remember her telling me that while visiting a cousin she was sitting on a porch swing, and he kept coming around with a fast horse and buggy! When they were married he was disinherited, and because he was only twenty, and not of age, his family claimed and took away his business — the only ice house in the small town where they lived. I believe it was Magnolia, Mississippi. Later, taking her with him to Texas, he worked for the Wells Fargo Railroad. When she became pregnant with my mother, her first child, she was desperately ill and he brought her back to his family home in Mississippi. They were told they could not stay there. So proud as he was he went to her father, Robert Ford Boutwell, who was a logging/sawmill camp boss. They remained there until my mother was born.

From the time I was almost five until I was almost thirteen, I lived in my grandparents' house in Meridian, Mississippi. I never considered it odd that I had two mothers, a Mommy and a Mother, and until I was a very big girl I thought that my Little Mama was my grandmother. Actually, she was my great-grandmother.

The happiest memories of my childhood are in that old frame house on the corner of 25th Avenue and 12th Street in Meridian, Mississippi. My mother and I shared a bedroom, papered to this day in pink-flowered wallpaper with some of the panels misshapen. The paper hanger was tipsy and my grandfather threw him out of the house, only later to demand he return and complete the job.

Because my grandmother was certain I was ready to go to school, I began when I was five years old. I first attended school at the Oakland Heights Elementary School, which was a wooden building. My first grade teacher was Miss Cathy. I do not recall Miss Cathy's first name, but it was she who taught me my colors and numbers and listened to me read aloud.

School years were rather uneventful. I had a library card — I can't remember when I did not have a card. My grandmother thought all well brought up children should have a reading background. Before I was in the second grade I had finished Black Beauty, Heidi, and many other children's classics. When words were too difficult I referred to the dictionary. I was the only child in an entire family of grown-up persons. There was no T.V., but there were wonderful radio programs and lots of books.

I suppose my most important memories are about the women in my family. My mother was a perfect mother — kind, good, and patient. Her mistake was in marrying a man who was simply not cut out to be her husband. He was jolly and kind when he was sober. There are many family stories about his betrayal of my mother, yet she loved him fiercely. When I was thirteen we left Meridian and moved to Birmingham because mother wanted us to "be a family." She had worked in a department store during those years we lived with my grandparents, and what little she earned was subsidized by my grandparents.

I was encouraged to be competitive in school and good grades were a must. I never remember being told to not attempt anything. I was told I should always be a lady, and I was taught that community and church work were the most important tasks of any citizen. I was raised a Southern Baptist and gave my testimony at 25th Avenue Baptist Church when I was eleven years old. I was baptized in that church.

Because she had not completed high school herself (a fact not known by many people), my grandmother placed a very high value on education. Her own children were educated and she intended for me to have as fine an education as possible. She was articulate and well-read herself.

On Saturdays I was allowed to walk downtown to the Temple Theatre and attend the Saturday double feature. Sometimes I could go to the Royal Theatre, but the preference was the Temple. The reason for this was that my grandmother knew the manager and the woman who ran the concession stand. Once I lost my quarter, and when this was discovered the lady told me to "go on in, Jane Lynn; I'll see Hazel at the Eastern Star tonight," and she handed me a quarter of her money. Twenty-five cents was the cost of a 10 cent ticket, 15 cents for ice cream and a comic book (Wonder Woman, of course).

During spring breaks and fall planting times I accompanied my grandmother in her big black Buick automobile laden with good-ies from the city stores to the family farm, to see and visit with the Boutwell branch of the family. The main Boutwell farm was very large. I have faint memories of Papa Boutwell, his handlebar mustache and his fox hounds and horses. I recall that once he held me on his shoulders and said to me, "Jane Lynn, look all the way around you — all the land you see for as far as you can see is Boutwell land."

Yet, it is the farm and the women who remain foremost in my mind.

The big farm was Little Mama's and Papa's house, and the sons held the two largest pieces of the land and worked them. My grandmother had the smallest piece of land, it was 80 acres. Although it was sold long ago, my grandmother's sons still hold the mineral rights to the land.

The big farmhouse was a wonderful one-level structure surrounded by a fenced yard filled with every kind of flower imaginable. A bell that was rung to bring the hands in from the field was in the side yard by the kitchen. A large well porch was on one side of the house and a screened day porch on the other. A hall ran the length of the house, and just to the left inside the front door was the parlor, furnished with rattan furniture, a huge radio, and a gramophone. A front porch ran the width of the house front. In the early days the house was heated by the brick fireplaces in each room, and in the evenings the light was provided by the wonderful oil lamps — the kind that had shades and gave light like our electric ones of today. An outhouse took care of those human needs.

The kitchen was big and light. I can close my eyes and smell the aroma of strong coffee and biscuits now. The kitchen had a fireplace that my Little Mama used even after electricity was available. The stove in earlier days was an enamel woodstove with a water reservoir and a hooded warmer above. Meals were filling and good. A large pantry opened off the kitchen and was stocked with every kind of home-canned vegetable and fruit, jelly and preserves. A hole cut in the floor in one corner and covered with a canvas was where scrapings from the table were poured into a bucket for the pigs. And it's where the many cats on the farm came and went as they pleased.

Later, indoor plumbing and running water were added along with the electricity and butane gas. The electric well pump was a community happening; my Grandfather Middleton (Big Daddy) brought it in the back of his pickup truck from the railroad delivery in Meridian to the farm. He and his two brothers-in-law worked for two days to install it. When it was primed and began to pump water, everyone for miles around came to see it run and use the taps.

Harvest times were the best! The tenant farmers and the Boutwell family worked very hard with the harvest. All of us, and especially the children, enjoyed the meals: huge platters of boiled corn, fried green tomatoes, boiled potatoes with green beans, cornbread (made in lots of large skillets with leftovers for the dogs), plenty of fresh butter and iced tea.

Until the electricity came, large iceboxes (filled with ice by an iceman who delivered twice a week from the nearest icehouse) kept things cool. Behind the house and down the hill was a crystal clear ground spring, its bubbles rising to the surface slowly. This spring was contained in a spring box that resembled a sandbox filled with cold water instead of sand. Into this spring box were lowered crocks of butter, milk, and anything else that needed refrigeration. Even in winter it was used. The children waded in the stream which was created and perpetuated by its overflow. On hot, hot days it surely felt good. Small crayfish scurried around in its sandy waters and the fun was in catching them.

The farm was a working farm. It not only provided vegetables but also dairy products and beef cattle. Life was fairly self-contained. Down the road one way was the church that had no regular pastor. A circuit preacher arrived once a month and on other Sundays one of the deacons officiated. I remember meetings to pray for rain and for deliverance from taxes.

The black sharecroppers (there must have been three or four families) were accepted and worked had and well. Disturbances were settled or rather arbitrated by the menfolk in the Boutwell family.

I suppose one could say that I enjoyed the best of two worlds; rural life and ease, and city education and social graces.

Holidays for the Middletons were grand occasions, especially Christmas. A big cedar tree reached the ceiling. It was so big that to hang the lights Big Daddy had to stand on a stepladder, and with directions from Mommy, wound them around the tree.

One particular Christmas stands out in my mind. In addition to the boxes of canned goods sitting on the floor of the big kitchen in the back of the house, there were boxes of secondhand clothing.

Mommy's Eastern Star and Sunday School class always prepared these for needy children.

This one Christmas was different. We had received a call from my Uncle Ford telling us that an old black woman named Bertha, who had worked and farmed with our Boutwell family for years, was very ill and needed to go to Meridian for treatment. Taking me with her for company, Mommy went to see about the situation.

Upon arriving at the farm, old Bertha was tenderly settled onto the back seat of the car where pillows and quilts had been placed for her comfort. Back home again, Mommy and Big Daddy took her to the Mattie Hersey Hospital, a charity hospital, where she was admitted. The next few days were filled with soft whispers and clucking in worry about her condition. Then, Mommy and I went to visit her at the charity hospital. It was the first time I had seen a charity ward and I have never forgotten it. I recall shiny linoleum floors, rows of beds filled with pained black faces against the white linens, white screens on rollers beside some beds, and at the very end next to the last was was my beloved Bertha. This was the Bertha who had made me candy, slipped me honey in a spoon, washed in a black pot in the yard, and heated flatirons on the hearth. She was very happy to see us and so appreciative. We told her we would be back soon to take her home. Mommy assured her that she had told the doctors that everyone must be home and settled before Christmas, and they were.

I do believe that the greatest things instilled in me during this time were the values that my Mommy held so dear. She belonged to many civic and social clubs including the Eastern Star, the Rebel Club (trainmen's auxiliary — the Rebel was a passenger train), the B&PW Club, the Women's Voters' League; and she took an active part in her church. She worked with the polls in elections until about eight years ago. She never turned away a caller at her door. There was never a need so great that she did not try to see to it or help solve it. She was prim and to some who did not truly understand her, she seemed cold, unfeeling. She was not given to hysteria, slobbering all over everybody, nor was she known for a soft spoken manner. Her criticism was sharp — a word of praise also found its way. One realized pleasing her was a great accomplishment.

As a grown lady now, I understand her reasoning in trying so hard to teach the girls in the family (there were four granddaughters) not to marry too young and to gain a good education to better care for themselves. I believe she was a victim of the times in which she lived. She lived during a Depression, had little education, no knowledge of birth control, and found herself often trapped by her own body and circumstances. She had a firm determination that we would fare better.

The years from my thirteenth birthday, when we left her home and came to Birmingham to be with my father, were like nightmares. I married at seventeen and she was so bitterly disappointed she did not send me a wedding gift until my first wedding anniversary. She sent a complete linen chest with monogrammed sheets and pillowcases. I was married three and a half years before my son was born when I was twenty. He was the first boy in the Middleton family in three generations.

Several days before my twenty-first birthday I received a letter. It is sad for me to recall that I no longer have it. Inside with the letter was a check signed by her for $5.00; the letter telling me to register to vote and pay my poll tax. One sentence is in my memory forever. It read, "Jane Lynn, I cannot bear the thought that for the want of the $5.00 fee my first grandchild, who happened to have been born female, should be denied the right we fought so hard to achieve." I registered to vote.

Perhaps I will never have the life she would have planned for me, but I do know that all whose lives touched hers were never diminished by so doing. When I die, if someone says about me what was said regarding her, then I will be a satisfied soul in whatever lies hereafter. One of her oldest friends said to me, "Jane Lynn, she loved her family, she loved people. Hazel's great blessing was love and loyalty. She was more than a good Christian or a good mother, she was a good person."

MICHAEL DAVID SHRADER

Tuscumbia, Alabama

Dr. Whitman had no children of his own. He tried with all his heart and soul to encourage me to become a physician. He would invite me to come and visit him at his office every day after school. His clinic was upstairs over the Palace Drugstore on the corner of Main Street, where the railroad cut through town.

Doc Whitman was the only college graduate in our whole church. He possum hunted with his friends, fished every week somewhere, and loved to sing in a rich second tenor all the old songs out of the Broadman hymnal.

He was over six feet tall and kept his rich brown hair close-cropped. He wore either a dark brown or dark blue suit all the time, except when he was fishing.

I was a very impressionable twelve years old when Whitman began to teach me how to doctor. His waiting room was right next to his treatment room. Some days in the summer he would leave the door open, and two twelve-inch black GE fans rotated in one-hundred-degree heat. In the treatment room there were two large glass cabinets loaded with every kind of gleaming tool and knife and a small sterilizer that stood within reach of the examination table. Doc's operating chair was a big steel chair with arms that adjusted, and a headrest with a big strap that fit down over the forehead. There were also arm straps that held the wrists tight. A big gooseneck lamp with a mirror reflector made the patient's face light up in exactly the spot where Doc was working.

Doc would sit on a small round stool in front of his patient, screw the stool seat up or down to fit his needs, and begin. The chair adjusted three ways: a patient could be tilted upside down, stood straight up, or just left horizontal, depending on the kind of work the doctor was doing. Two big adjustable stirrups stuck out of the lower end. He would examine the women of the surrounding hills by draping them with a sheet after some member of the woman's family or a female neighbor had undressed her. Then with the other women standing around he would walk in in his stiffly starched white coat, with his headpiece reflector in place, put on rubber gloves out of a sterile package, and while the other women watched with sober curiosity, he would begin his examination.

I asked him why he insisted on having family members help with his work, instead of using Miss Louella, his secretary and nurse. He told me that kept down trouble, reduced fear of examination, and taught other women how to be good patients, all at the same time.

By the end of the summer of 1943, I had learned how to set down symptoms and how to look them up, how to set bones, sew up cuts, stop off bleeders, and use most of Doc's many tools. He had me teaching a first aid course to the ladies at the community center who rolled bandages for the Red Cross. I had even learned to do small fancy stitches and tie off catgut so it wouldn't slip, and by August I was Doc's chief assistant at the county and city jails. We had plenty of sewing practice on Friday and Saturday nights.

After I'd been hanging around all summer, Doc got the bright idea that he would train me to remove tonsils. He had a young boy patient from the orphan's home over in Hatton that had bad tonsils, and he scheduled him to have his operation Thursday morning. The little boy was already on the table in the office when we came in. Miss Louella had put him in a gown and had given him one of Doc's sleeping pills. Doc laughed and talked to the little boy for a few minutes and then described to him how we were going to fix his badly infected tonsils.

For two weeks prior to the operation Doc had used some of the new drug called penicillin to try to reduce the swelling and infection. The new stuff had worked so well that most of the pus and swelling had gone and the tonsils looked almost normal.

We laid the patient down on the operating chair and put a small cone over his nose and mouth, and then began to drop ether onto the cone straight out of a can. The little boy was quickly asleep.

The doctor sat him back up and we began to fix him in a tonsil position. First we used a pair of large clamps with reverse screws on them to keep his sagging mouth pried wide open. I had a new electric-powered suction pump that kept sucking the saliva out of his mouth and out of the way. We used three simple tools to remove the tonsils: a long steel stick with a corkscrew on one end, a longer steel stick with a small razor sharp single-edge blade, and a funny-looking device that resembled a skeletal pistol with a loop at the end of the gunbarrel.

The way Doc taught me to do tonsils was first to swab the edge of the throat gently with a mixture of iodine, merthiolate, and calendula; then ease the corkscrew straight into the tonsil and pull up gently on it, until it bulged out like an oyster coming out of its shell. Then I'd gently slice the membrane holding the tonsil down to the throat, freeing it. Next I'd slide the wire loop right over the steel rod and carefully position it on the stem of the tonsil and pull the trigger . . . and out came the tonsil. I was hell on tonsils before I was fifteen.

But I quit trying to learn medicine after poems started coming into my head. I told Doc Whitman about the voice that spoke so beautifully to me about so many things. He encouraged me to write down what the voice said and not to be concerned about doctoring.

That's how I started being a poet.

ESSIE STALLWORTH McGOWIN

❧ ❧ ❧

Pineville, Alabama

I was born in Ennis, Texas, but my father had gone there from Mobile after the end of the War Between the States. Opportunities were so limited in the deep South after the war that my father succumbed to the lure of the Southwest. After a few years, when my sister Stella and I were little girls, he feel for the glamour of Claremont and the silver mines of New Mexico. This was Indian territory, about which he knew nothing. Nevertheless, in 1883, we said goodbye to friends and neighbors and went to Claremont.

Toward the end of the first year, a man and his wife came to live with us and help on the ranch. It was fifteen miles over rugged trails to the nearest post office and twelve miles to the cabin of our neighbor. The only visitors to our ranch were cowboys or prospectors looking for silver. At times straggling groups of Mexicans came by; anyone to break the monotony was welcome.

My mother, who was always beautiful and joyous, went about her tasks with a worried look. Her two little girls were without anything that civilization brings and she was expecting another baby. She knew she would never live through it and selected a spot in a little grove where she wished to be buried.

When the time came on October 3, 1884, it was difficult to get a doctor, and when he did arrive there was little he could do. All day long we hovered around utterly forlorn, hearing the heartbreaking moaning behind the closed door. We had never been shut out before. Late in the afternoon Papa called us to him and by the kitchen fire told us she was gone. They placed her in a hollowed-out trunk of a tree for a coffin with the baby, Carol Latimer, in her arms. In the grove at the spot she had selected they were laid to rest.

Stella and I lived in a world we created. It was peopled with friends, cousins, aunts, and uncles we had left behind in the "real world." We named the cattle for them and when a lonesome lowing came over the hills we would say, "that's cousin Molly."

One day, Stel, who was three years older than me, stood in the doorway brushing her long blonde hair, when suddenly our big shepherd dog began barking furiously and rushed toward the gate. Stel followed him and suddenly screamed, "Indians!" I looked up from my book and saw the barrels of three guns pointed at me. Their faces were daubed with red paint and red and blue strings were twisted in their hair. Their wide belts had cartridges and a large assortment of knives.

One look was enough for me. I made a wild dash for the bedroom and scrambled under the bed. Stel rushed in and locked the door. My father, who was ill that day, ran out onto the porch in time to see the Indians running toward the corral with Shep at their heels. A bullet came from the corral and he fell. Another bullet struck Father in the arm. Father and the housekeeper were in the stockroom preparing our defense. The firing was getting heavy and Stel was afraid. She wanted to be with Papa and made a dash for the stockroom door. A bullet came close, it singed her hair.

All day there were intermittent shots, not directed at any target, but probably hoping to run us out. The kitchen door was riddled. Gradually, the firing grew lighter and by sundown all was quiet.

We dared not make a fire and we had had nothing to eat since breakfast. Father and Chestly sawed portholes in the three exposed sides of the kitchen and kept vigil with loaded guns while we slept.

The next morning the place was deadly still, no sound except cattle lowing. Every horse was gone and some cattle had been killed. There was nothing to do but wait. Surely someone would come to find us, we thought. For three days we waited. On the fourth day three horsemen came over the ridge. They had picks and shovels tied to their saddles and looked at us in amazement. The leader said, "We were sent to bury you."

Now, the problem was to get the six of us away. They got us three horses and there were nine people in all. We dared not leave until dark, but had a hurried supper. As twilight lengthened into darkness, we closed the doors of our home, took one last look at the grave of our mother, and went out into the night.

Progress was slow through the darkness and the mountains were so steep I had a horrible fear that I would make a misstep and go rolling down the mountainside and no one would hear me. I would clutch at tall grass, rocks, anything to steady my steps. I walked awhile and then was taken up to ride behind one of the men. It was agony to keep awake.

Stella could guide a horse and they would let her ride alone. It was near midnight and would soon be time for a rest and a snack when I heard someone call, "Where's Stella?"

Stella was missing. We had crossed a stream some distance back and the first thought was that maybe she couldn't get across. The men fanned out in a half circle, while father made straight for the stream. I crouched in the darkness and tried to think of life without Stel.

Then footsteps approached. Did they find her? Yes, and a frightened little girl she was. Her horse had stopped at the stream to drink and in the darkness she had lost her way. She dared not shout since any kind of noise was prohibited. All she could do was cry and hope someone would come and find her.

Once we saw a flare up on the mountain top and an answering flare go up on a mountain nearby. Father said we were in the valley and these were signals. Indians with their keen sense of hearing could hear us passing below and they were sending information to the ones ahead.

The night wore slowly on and at last, when the first rays of the morning sun came up over the mountains, we rode into the little town of Alma.

The women of Alma took us in and made us the clothes we would need on the trip to Alabama. We waited three weeks for the train from Silver City. During that time hardly a day passed without a funeral, as there was still fighting with the bands of Apache Indians.

Finally our chance came. A train of covered wagons taking ore from the mines to the refinery in Silver City let us ride in one of the wagons. It was 65 miles and the nine wagons in the train had to go very slowly. Water was the greatest problem and the Indians knew the spot of each water hole. They tried to reach one of these each noon and night. One noon we found coals still smoking and moccasin prints around the water hole. If we hadn't been late there would have been no more of us.

One afternoon we drove into a little settlement and made plans to camp there for the night. The headman invited us into his home. In the backyard was a row of about eight or nine cottages or cabins. Each child pointed out which one he or she lived in. Their mothers were sewing and tending babies. The wife in the main house had cookies and milk for all of the children. This was a Mormon village.

In 1885 we arrived in Pineville, Monroe County, Alabama, to live with our grandparents. Both my father's and mother's families lived there, but we stayed with my father's people, the Stallworths.

GOULD BEECH

Montgomery, Alabama

I was five and my sister, Delia, was two. We were playing on the floor of the wide hallway near the front door of my Grandmother Means' home in Boligee, Alabama. There were other relatives there — my favorite cousin, Al Burch, and his mother. Grandmother Means was dabbing at her eyes with a handkerchief, but I do not remember any words. Just a hushed sadness.

The next morning my father arrived. I remember the two of us walking along the dirt road to my aunt's house, hand in hand. He was trying to tell me that my mother was dead. The year was 1918, the year of the great influenza epidemic which took the lives of thousands.

The day of the funeral it was raining — a pouring, drenching late October rain. The casket was in the living room of my aunt's house. I remember standing by an older cousin, also named Delia, who was about 13, and I could see the tears rolling down her cheeks while the minister read the service. Six men carried the casket to a one-mule wagon. The wagon belonged to Fax, who was born a slave. (The nearest hearse was in Eutaw, ten miles of slippery, black muck away, and it could not come.)

Four men in raincoats carried the coffin to the wagon with the help of my father and the minister. Fear of colds and influenza kept even family members from coming that day, and only the men went to the cemetery.

I have been told that the impact of such a trauma could be the reason why I have no memories before that day. My only memory of my mother is from photographs and what others have told me about her: she was sweet, gentle, and happy. But I do not recall a touch, a word, a glimpse of her.

And so my life — so far as memory is concerned — began with this sadness. I grew up shy and sensitive.

Grandmother, Delia Thornton Gould Means, was a gentle and genteel Presbyterian — she left the Episcopal Church to join with her husband when she married at 19. Though he died in 1891, she remained a devout Presbyterian in deference to his memory. While she wore light grey or blue gingham dresses in the summer time, her winter dresses were black or dark grey — usually with a little white lace around the collar. She never left the house without a corset.

After grandfather's death, she managed to raise two daughters and three sons — her earnings as a post office clerk supplemented the small rent from 90 acres of none-too-productive farm land. In later years, she received a Confederate pension of $16 a month from the State of Alabama. With the farm rental, the total could not have been more than $25 a month. Yet she never mentioned the lack of money as being a hardship, and was still doing her housework when she died at 79. The four-poster beds, rectangular grand piano, dark walnut dining table with the patina of several generations of use, and a nine-foot-high bookcase-secretary were reminders of better days gone by.

Her brother, McKee Gould, who was called "Buddy" by everyone in town, had inherited their family home, the "Hill of Howth." Built of square-hewn logs in 1912, its floors were not at all level. But there was an aura about it that gave me exquisite pleasure every time I entered it. The cross-cut saw and adze used in its construction were behind the front door.

Buddy would take me up to the attic to explore from time to time on Sunday afternoons. There were stacks of neatly-bundled copies of *The National Intelligencer*, a daily newspaper published in Washington. There were also bound volumes of the *New York Daily Mirror* and *Ladies Literary Digest*. William Proctor Gould, who had built the house with his commanding officer, Colonel John McKee, had come south during the period when the Indians were being forced to leave Alabama. *The National Intelligencer* was still arriving the day Fort Sumter was fired on.

Twenty-two volumes of Gould's daily journals and diary were in a bookcase, and Buddy would let me borrow one at a time to read. The dates of planting corn and cotton, the rainfall and temperature and crop yields were recorded. Eight senior slaves had a designated acre each and an exact record of their yields and the money they received was also kept. The illness of a family member or slave was the subject of daily entries, along with the medications given. Gould was opposed to Alabama's secession, but joined in support of the Confederate cause.

My sister and I lived with Grandmother Means during the summers. When I was eight, I was watching Buddy as he and a crew of men were baling hay. "Gould, would you like to have a job?" I was elated — watching was fun, being part of the process was exhilarating. My assignment: to keep the mule, which supplied the power for compressing the hay, going in a circle. The mule was hitched to a long pole which was geared to the baler, and if not tapped or urged on from time to time, would stop. On Saturday, when the job was finished after I had been there two days, Buddy handed me three quarters and a dime. It was the most money I had ever had, and the first I had earned at a meaningful job.

Boligee had five general stores, a drug store, a filling station, and a black honky-tonk. (The music of a loud piano could be heard as one passed the honky-tonk and I always wished I could go in.) On the Saturday I got paid, I went to two stores before finding an aluminum boiler that could be bought for 65 cents. A con-artist salesman had told grandmother that enamel boilers were bad for your health because you might swallow an enamel chip.

Naturally, grandmother was overcome when I gave her this token of my love. Later, my interest in cooking utensils led to one of the few occasions when she upbraided me. The subject was the relative merits of cast-iron skillets and the thin steel skillets. She said it was a waste of money to buy a steel skillet. I replied, "Colored people buy steel skillets all the time — they must be dumb."

"Son," she spoke to me firmly and with a note of disapproval. "Don't ever say they're dumb. They just don't have the money to buy good skillets."

Neither grandmother nor any of the women in the family ever used the word "nigger," and only occasionally can I remember a man using the term when provoked or angry. The ties of black and white families were such that most blacks had a protector in time of need.

I never heard of anyone in the Boligee area belonging to the 1920's emergence of the Ku Klux Klan. Paternalism was the pattern, and whites were motivated to make life at least tolerable — otherwise who would plant, chop, and pick cotton? The latter-day Klan was made up mostly of rednecks, but its leadership included many small businessmen, and some God-fearing preachers outraged by the era of bootlegging, short skirts, jazz, and the Charleston.

The black-to-white ratio in Greene County was eight-to-one. The pattern of life was probably closer to the "plantation days" of the pre-Civil War era than in any other county in the state. Most of the land, all the stores, gins, filling stations, and the bank were owned by whites. I recall a black barber, the operator of the juke joint, a well-driller, a preacher, two teachers, and Aunt Sally Bouchelle's yardman-chauffeur, the only black males not dependent on farming.

Blacks and whites lived in two separate worlds, even though they were in constant daily contact. Each knew much about the other. Yet there was so much that neither knew. There were hundreds of unwritten rules and regulations that governed the conduct of both. No black, for example, could address any adult white without the use of some title: Mister, Mizez, Miss, Captain, Professor, and so on. And no white could use any title in addressing a black until age made appropriate Uncle or Aunt.

Just about everybody in Boligee was kin to everybody else — or there were marriages that tied one family to another. There was one white family that remained on the outside. The father had been a sawmill hand. The boys in the family had a measure of acceptance by their peers, but the daughters were shunned. Not for any moral reason, but because they were "different." Their dresses were different, their shoes were different, they looked different. I thought from time to time about the pains they must have felt when they were not invited to picnics and barbecues.

One of the privileges that came to a boy of twelve was going with the men to the camphouse on the Tombigbee River the night before big barbecues. Before dark there was oak and hickory wood to be cut and brought to the location of the fire. The fire was located 15 or 20 feet away from the pit and was started early to build up a supply of red-hot coals.

The pit itself was about five feet across and 15 or 20 feet long — it was dug down to a depth of about a foot. A half calf, a middle-size pig, and a mutton were the usual fare for a July 4 outing. Long, skinned poles were wired to the carcasses, and a man on either end would turn the meat over from time to time. Cooking began about 11 at night. Coals from the fire were sprinkled under the meat by one of the men who knew how to keep the heat at the right temperature. Boys could sop on the sauce with a sopping stick — a piece of old sheet was tied to the end of the stick and dipped in an iron pot which was kept hot. The sauce was made of butter, lemon juice or vinegar, and salt and pepper. I was grown before I ever heard of anybody burdening barbecue sauce with catsup or tomato sauce. By 2:00 a.m. everybody would be asleep except one or two of the men who took turns at the pit.

Corn baked in its shuck was the favorite accompaniment — sweet potatoes, potato salad and green salad were brought by the women and girls who arrived the morning of the feast. Never have I tasted anything as good as that barbecue and fixins. Then again, never since have I been a child.

HUBERT GRISSOM, JR.

❦ ❦ ❦

Cullman, Alabama

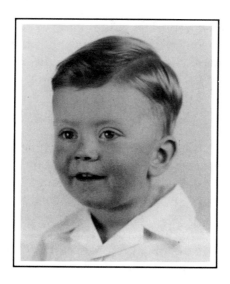

Paw Paw would not have wanted me to attend his funeral. I knew that, he knew that, and I knew he knew. But he was dead. So I quietly left Camp Westmoreland on the backwaters of the Tennessee near Florence, Alabama, with Uncle Orval, on the day before I was to get my thumb pricked and enter the Brotherhood of the Order of the Arrow.

Years after his death, I learned that the townsfolk of Cullman, Alabama, called Paw Paw "Uncle Sam." His given name was Benjamin Franklin Hembree, and in the early part of this century he went with a degree from Jacksonville State to Cullman to become a school teacher. But he soon learned that he could make more money delivering the mail.

So he became Uncle Sam and walked Route Number One in downtown Cullman. He walked it with his leather pouch slung over his shoulder with a smile and a good word for everyone. The day after I received my Eagle Scout badge, I sat in the barber's chair getting my crew cut. I sat with my tongue out and folded between my teeth, a sign of determination I live with to this day. Such a habit has not served me well: I damn near lost my tongue to Steve Griffith's elbow during football practice at Cullman High School, and when getting a crew cut in the mid-1950s small flicks of hair would land on my tongue . . . again not exactly pleasant.

On that day, Paw Paw came into the barber shop, handing out mail from his pouch, speaking and smiling to everyone. He made a beeline to the second chair where I sat, and said in a voice that was uncustomarily loud, "I'll trade my college degree for that Eagle Scout Badge of yours." I swelled up at least twice my size under the striped barber's apron.

Cheerleading my education was something Paw Paw had always done.

While getting my basket-weaving merit badge, it fell my duty to weave a chair bottom. When the hemp got near the middle and the coil would no longer go through the diamond weave, I'd take the end of the hemp and run it from my front yard past the sweet gum tree, past the long leaf pine and Paw Paw's showcase garden down to his two story house, turn around at his automobile-sized boxwood, and return to the chair bottom to run the hemp through the weave. Then I'd travel east through Aunt Teen's yard, down toward the Moore's house where they had a pump organ and a hand-carved chest from far off India. I made several of those trips one day while Paw Paw hoed his garden and circles of sweat appeared at the arm pits of his long-sleeved grey work shirt.

If he laughed, I never knew it. All I remember was his leaning on the handle-end of his hoe and admiring my chair bottom as I flipped it over and put the final knot in my basket-weaving merit badge.

Paw Paw took *Progressive Farmer* and his weed-free garden was the one folks drove by on a Sunday afternoon just to look at. My first connection with Paw Paw's garden happened when I was about two and a half. Story has it that I wandered down one of the rows, where I found a friendly king snake. Apparently we got along just fine, for

I picked it up and let it coil itself around me. Come to think about it, maybe the king snake found me. But anyway, we became good friends and as I walked (or toddled) toward the house I'm reported to have looked up to the second story window to Mother's room and said, "Nake, Mama! Nake!" My memory serves me well enough to hear to this day her bloodcurdling scream.

Paw Paw, his garden, and his and Maw Maw's house were very much a part of my early education.

First, the garden. The back two rows next to the pasture grew strawberries that seemed much more trouble to raise than snake-handling babies. The berry plants, back during those Strawberry Festival days in Cullman, took two years to produce. In the spring of their second year Paw Paw and I would kneel almost prayerfully at each plant and carefully cradle each little berry on dry pine straw. Then we'd build scarecrows to keep the birds away. Sometimes the scarecrows were funny, but they always had pie pans that would clamor in the wind of those soft spring days.

When the corn was finger size, Paw Paw taught me to thin it with a hoe. And when with a determined tongue tuck I went into the garden to harvest okra without a shirt on, I never heard Paw Paw's laughter . . . but it was probably there. One shirtless trip in between two rows of okra taught me why Paw Paw wore that long-sleeved grey work shirt in his garden on the hottest summer days.

Paw Paw sectioned his in-town farm and gave a lot to each of his four children. The garden was on Uncle Buell's lot because Uncle Buell ended up in Seattle helping design airplanes for Boeing. My bedroom window overlooked the garden and the sculptured hedge that separated the garden from Maw Maw's and Paw Paw's house. And, during those summer months of all-vegetable meals and hot fresh cornbread, I could, after the food was on the table, dash out to the edge of the garden and pluck small peppers before they got too hot.

Paw Paw was always the first person in town to stalk his tomato plants. The two rows were just north of the path that ran from our backyard to the apple tree near Paw Paw's tool shed. After a summer of eating large, red, perfect tomatoes and giving tomatoes to family, friends, and other folks, there were still enough for something like seventy gallons of tomato juice that sat at the bottom of the basement stairs, white on the top and settling deep red on the bottom. That tomato juice was still there when I was in college . . . years after a drunk wandered onto Paw Paw's land and killed him.

And when the green onions became more than we could eat or give away, Paw Paw and I would wash them and bunch them, and he'd let me walk the block or so to South Park Grocery and sell them for a dime that sat large and comfortable in my bluejeans pocket.

Paw Paw seemed to treat all his grandchildren differently. And while I'm sure he was a teacher to all of us, I always felt singled out for my education. One year, while Paw Paw was shopping at the Hill Grocery, he bought me six rose bushes and some gladiola bulbs. After telling me how, Paw Paw watched me plant, fertilize, and water the rose bushes and bulbs. I guess of all the plants Paw Paw loved roses the best. A blanket of the deepest red roses lay over his coffin in the living room in front of the glassed-in bookshelves that contained *National Geographics* going back to issue number one when they were pamphlet-sized.

On a rainy day, Paw Paw's and Maw Maw's house was an education in and of itself. We could, through the *National Geographics*, travel to far off jungles and giggle at the bare-breasted women, or locate India where the Moores got their hand-carved chest.

Upstairs, where my mother, her sister and brothers grew up, there was an angled attic full of World War II mementos . . . a picture of Uncle Buell's submarine, a Japanese sword, the Santa Claus suit that one of us wore each Christmas to hand out the presents . . . and Clifford's many war medals. Clifford and his sister lost their parents while growing up, and Maw Maw and Paw Paw moved them into the upstairs and they became a part of the family.

The dining room downstairs was a focal point of family life. Each Sunday afternoon after church and after the dishes were cleared from the table, Paw Paw, the longtime treasurer of the First Methodist Church, would spread the table with an old tablecloth and there the grandchildren could help him count the money and roll the coins for the Lord.

The backyard was important too. Paw Paw filled in the well and we made a circled flower garden planted with King Alfred daffo-dils. The backyard was where we hand-cranked ice cream, and where they had a family reunion once and entertained the preacher. The youngest grandchild was put on the ice cream crank just before it set-up and became impossible to turn.

Even more important than the living room circled with *National Geographics*, the adventuresome upstairs, penny-rolling dining room and the backyard, was the enclosed back porch with its metal glider and porcelain-topped table where Paw Paw kept his best seeds for next year's garden. After supper we grandchildren had the option of going to that back porch, and sitting on the glider where Paw Paw would read us the "Kon Tiki" or tell of his trip to Alaska. On the way home each night the path that ran through the garden was usually bright silver . . . dew covered, moonlit and cool underfoot . . . and it was anywhere on this blue, green earth we wanted it to be . . . or more precisely where Paw Paw had taken us that evening.

One morning before Sunday School, I stood outside the First Methodist Church staring at the handsome, hand-quarried sandstone and the deep hues of the stained glass windows, thinking that an hour of Sunday School, another hour of church, an hour of or so of rolling pennies, and then an hour of vespers might be a little too much toil in the vineyards of the Lord. Paw Paw pulled up in his 1948 Chevrolet, opened the door for Maw Maw, saw her to the door, then walked up to me to ask how my merit badges were coming along. He read my mind. "It's such a pretty day," he said, let's walk down to People's Drugstore and get us an ice cream cone. They won't miss us in Sunday School." I got strawberry, Paw Paw got vanilla, and we walked back to the First Methodist Church in time to enter the family pew which was two rows from the front and on the righthand side. Paw Paw always sat on the end of the pew near the bright stained glass window, so it'd be convenient for him to walk to the altar and receive the collection plates from the ushers.

Paw Paw took me with him to Mobile for a postal convention once. And of course Maw Maw bought me a new pair of shoes. Paw Paw walked me all over Mobile . . . we walked down the waterfront where stevedores and sailors sat in bars drinking beer and whiskey openly (a shock since Cullman was dry) . . . and we walked out Government Boulevard to visit one of Paw Paw's brothers who was in the furniture business . . . we walked through the park . . . we walked and walked. That night at the banquet, blisters swelled in my new shoes as I ate my English peas, mashed potatoes, and chicken, and listened to the affairs of the United States Postal Service.

On the way back from Mobile that summer in Paw Paw's 1948 Chevrolet, he drove me to Cahaba and explained that it was the first capital of Alabama. We walked around the foundation of what was once a state building that sat quietly and solidly in the woods. Paw Paw seemed to measure his words so that everything that came out of his mouth was both entertaining and educational.

The folks of Cullman loved their Uncle Sam too. After Paw Paw was killed, they rushed Maw Maw to the University Hospital in Birmingham while the house on the corner filled up with food and flowers, and I was being retrieved from Camp Westmoreland. The flowers filled up the living room and dining room and overflowed to the front porch. The postal employees sent a flower-covered replica of a mailbox; on its open lid lay a deep purple orchid. When I went to the backyard to get flowers for Paw Paw's grave later that summer, the weeds had gotten to the roses he gave me, but the gladiolas were in full bloom.

The night I was to have my finger pricked and enter the Brotherhood of the Order of the Arrow, I sat on the edge of my bed smelling the fresh earth of Paw Paw's weed-free garden and staring at the house where Paw Paw lay under a blanket of deep red roses. But Paw Paw would have wanted me to be up there on the backwaters of the Tennessee River in my Indian outfit, getting my finger pricked, and not sitting there on the edge of the bed staring at a house filled with food and flowers . . . softly crying.

SMITH MOSELEY

🐦 🐦 🐦

Selma, Alabama

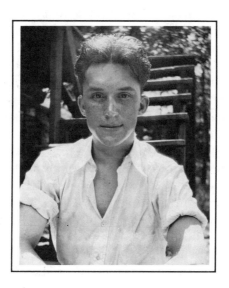

I n the carefree days when I was five, I adventured deep into that plantation country known as the Black Belt. Even now, more than half a century away, I can recall those days with a deep satisfaction and sense of Eden lost.

My domain included brooks and paths and pastures, fences and farms and animals and a black boy named Gabe to play with. Beyond the village were the unvisited far hills.

I remember the sounds and silences of those times. To this day the casual, contented clucking of hens in a barnyard — now seldom heard — carries with it a sense of well-being and a vast brooding tranquility. The far barking of a dog, the clip-clop of horses' hooves and the sound of buggy wheels on gravel were assurances that the bastions of my world were well-manned.

I recall few faces from this period. Aside from Gabe and my brother and my parents, other people were faceless and out of focus in my world, or so it seems from this distant point of view. But I remember Old Man Ullman. Some of what I remember I am sure I learned in later years from my mother, but most of my recollections are of his impact on my five-year-old mind, and for certain observations made as he moved austerely through those times.

Old Man Ullman was not really old. My informed guess is that he was in his middle fifties. He seemed to be always around his premises and if I had been more mature I would have wondered about his business, and how he sustained himself and his family. A casual comment of my mother's many years later answered this question with curious drama: Old Man Ullman, it seems, was an attorney, apparently an able and arrogant one. According to my mother, he one day lost a case. In disgust he locked his law office and went home for good.

Something about the man must have fascinated my child's mind for I am now vaguely aware that I followed him about a good deal. In this constant surveillance he must have found me as welcome as the plague. Perhaps he felt that my presence inhibited him in the full expression of the colorful profanity with which he purpled the neighborhood. If he exercised any restraint because of my big-eyed, big-eared nearness it was not noticeable to me.

Old Man Ullman swore with awesome abandon at everything that displeased him: a broken hoe, weeds in the garden, a stray dog, or a fugitive chicken. His face would darken with blood and the veins would stand out on his broad forehead while his gray hair shook under the force of the gathering storm. The voice that had thundered in the courtroom now roared in the barnyard and his outraged protests exploded in pyrotechnical blasphemy.

Small indeed were the circumstances that could trip the trigger of Old Man Ullman's ire. Literally, he went always fit-to-be-tied. But tied he was not and the village made allowance for him because that was "his way."

One thing in particular seem to annoy him out of all reason or understanding. It concerned the horses and a thing most natural and characteristic of horses. Daily he led these great patient beasts down to the creek for water. They thrust their velvet muzzles into the clear stream above the smooth white pebbles and made musical sucking noises as they drank. Those innocent, and to me, pleasant sounds, did something to Old Man Ullman. I never new why, but he fairly writhed in anger, running the entire gamut of his blasphemous repertoire and back again. The horses never seem to mind, except to cast a sideways glance at him under their long lashes. When they had finished and raised their heads Old Man Ullman led them patiently back to the barn, still muttering diminishing oaths. I told my mother about this curious habit and she suggested that perhaps I had better not go on these missions. But I did.

There came a day when summer lay somnolently on the land and the chickens clucked contentedly in the barnyard and wagons and buggies ground along the graveled road, and I, as usual, made small excursions about my world. Except for those natural sounds the day was dreamy and silent. Gabe was likely with me and we may have been sitting under the shade and talking about God and how He could throw that house across the river "with his lil fingah."

A shotgun roared. Sound and silence fled together and stood shivering against the far hills. For a moment there was a vacuum in the day when nothing moved and no sound was heard. Then a woman screamed. Suddenly there were people running or walking fast toward the Ullmans'. I saw my mother come out on the back steps, walking fast and resolutely. She saw me and said, "Don't follow me." She moved on toward the Ullmans' and now we could hear a woman crying. Gabe and I looked at each other with wondering eyes, feeling that our pleasant world had become suddenly threatened.

Now there were a great many people at the Ullmans' and some men were busy about the back steps, but we couldn't see what they were doing because of the vines that covered the fence. Another vehicle pulled by two black horses drew up in front of the house and Gabe sucked in his breath and his eyes grew bigger. "That the dead wagon," he said. Then he announced with finality, "Ahm goin' home," and he went.

I sat still, full of wonder and somehow vaguely depressed. I sat there for a long time until I saw my mother come out and start home, walking tall as always, but with a troubled face. I joined her, looking up questioningly at her. She took my hand but said nothing. When we reached the house she stood for a moment patting my shoulder and thinking. Then she said, "Mr. Ullman is dead. Now I have to bake a cake. You go out and play, but don't leave the yard." She reached for a mixing bowl and then stood thinking for a moment before she reached for the flour. I went outside, feeling uneasy and groping for comprehension of a world without Mr. Ullman.

During the rest of the day people came and went at the Ullmans', many with covered dishes, and in the late afternoon my mother went over taking the cake. By this time my brother had come in from school and that night he would tell me what he knew. He said Old Man Ullman had shot himself. Next day Gabe was around and in a guarded moment he would tell me far more graphically . . . "He blowed he haid off sittin' on the back steps."

I have no recollection of the funeral, to which, of course, I did not go. I am sure I must have seen the procession pass the house with the black hearse, followed by a stream of buggies and an occasional carriage. A day or so later Gabe would approach me mysteriously and after we were out of sight and earshot of the house he would tell me, big-eyed, that he had something to show me. "What?" I asked. "You come on," said Gabe. I followed the mysterious Gabe, and we crawled through some bushes and vines nearly to the fence behind the Ullman house. Gabe parted some brush and pointed. The corner of a pine box, partially buried, stuck out of the ground a few feet away. Gabe said with heavy drama, "There where they bury he brains." It never occurred to me to doubt the story. It may have been so.

JIM REED

Tuscaloosa, Alabama

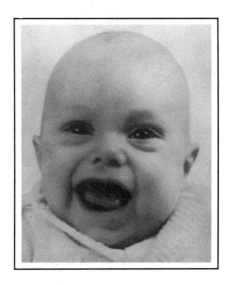

The streets of downtown Tuscaloosa smelled of tear gas the night Jack Palance was there. I missed the excitement because I had been working a night shift at WJRD radio. I sure heard about it, though. The only traces of what had happened remained in the deserted, quiet night air.

What I heard was that Jack Palance, the actor, on his way someplace else, had stopped in Tuscaloosa to stay the night. Rumor spread that he had been seen going into the Druid Theatre with a black woman. A crowd had apparently formed, unruliness was the rule and somebody had dispersed it with tear gas.

So much for welcoming celebrities to town in the early 1960s. It really doesn't matter what the press had to say about the incident. Doesn't really matter what each witness or near-witness said. Nobody seemed to have the whole story. In fact, the story was more important than the facts back then.

The mood of the times could be sensed rather than explained. Black people were getting uppity, spurred on by Yankees come to town to agitate. Most of us didn't know much more than that. We just stayed afraid that something bad was going to happen — either at the hands of rednecks or Negroes or Yankees. Or somebody.

I was a radio announcer back then. I got my WJRD job by going to see John Cooper, the station manager, on the advice of some of my radio friends. Up till then I had worked at WNPT in Northport and WUOA at the University. But WJRD in those days was hot stuff to us young aspiring broadcast personalities. WJRD was considered to be the "good music" station. That meant it played only Frank Sinatra and Mantovani-type music and catered to adults. Country and rock had still not taken hold of mainstream Tuscaloosa grownups.

The status job awaited me at WJRD. I didn't know then that the station was in severe financial trouble and that John Cooper was on his way out. All I knew is that I went to see him in his front office overlooking Kress and Broad Street.

"You know, Jim, one of the finest feelings in the world is standing in the woods all alone, peeing against a tree," said John Cooper in my interview. I don't really remember what else was said, but apparently I was already hired anyhow. He knew of my work and really seemed preoccupied with something.

It didn't take long for me to learn the ropes at WJRD. Most of the rules were unwritten. But one rule everybody was taught soon enough. John Birchard, a self-styled liberal announcer from New England studying at the University, spelled it out for me. "When we read the news, we cannot use the word 'Negro'," John said.

I remember saying something like, "Huh?"

John said, "Here are the rules: Saying 'Negro' is too dignified and would offend may of our listeners."

I said, "You mean we're supposed to call them —"

"Oh, no, we could never use the term 'Nigger,' since that would make us sound low-class," John continued. "It is proper to say,

'Nigra.' That is the way we're going to say it. Keeps us out of trouble with our sponsors."

"Do you follow the rules?" is what I wanted to ask John and the others, but I knew better. Everybody had to make up his or her own mind about how much trouble they wanted to stay in with John Cooper. John Birchard and other announcers were only temporary, anyhow, on their way to better places once they graduated. Back to Connecticut, New York, Virginia and other areas where they could go back to pretending to be liberals. Disdaining the South was very fashionable, both to Yankees when they got back home and to Southerners who wanted to be accepted by their Yankee friends.

A Yankee was anybody from the Northeast, the North, the Midwest, the West Coast, or any place north of Tennessee.

I knew I couldn't bring myself to use the words "Nigger" or "Nigra." But I also wanted to work at the most prestigious station in town. Back then, it was journalistic fashion for wire service writers, TV reporters, and newspapers to identify everybody in each story as either black or white. Yellow and red didn't seem to be necessary. If you were an Indian it wasn't mentioned. I'm part Cherokee, but I never heard a story that read, "Cherokee Jim Reed was appointed to a committee at the Veterans Hospital today." Being a Negro would certainly be important to the same story.

It was impossible to read a wire story (that's what we called all the news we delivered on the air, since we got it from the Associated Press or United Press International wire services) without running across race identifiers throughout the copy.

The solution to my problem was simple. And it kept me out of trouble with my bosses. I simply never read the word "Negro" or the term "black" when I delivered the news. Thus, "A black man was arrested for holding up the IGA grocery store today" became "A man was arrested for . . ."

No one ever knew about my silent rebellion. In the mind of the audience, the news was almost never about black people, anyhow. The normal Southern tendency is to picture all people in the news as being white unless they are identified as black.

Another thing I learned quickly was that no Negro music was allowed on the air at WJRD. It became evident that this meant no Negro-sounding music was allowed. To the listener's mind that translated as music in which the vocalist had a black dialect or a name strongly identified with black civil rights causes. This excluded just about everybody black. In the case of instrumental selections, the name of the band leader would have to be white or generally unrecognized as black. For instance, we could occasionally slip in a number by Count Basie because few white listeners knew he was black.

Nat King Cole was *the* exception to all the rules. We could play Nat King Cole all day and never get into trouble. That's because Nat King Cole was loved by female listeners, especially, and tolerated by most men. Until the civil rights movement heated up in the mid and late sixties, Nat King Cole had a wide following in Alabama. You could even say his name on the air, which really broke the color barriers. For instance, we could play black performers' songs on the air if they didn't *sound* black and if we didn't announce their names. Saved again from the wrath of listeners and John Cooper. Nat King Cole romanced the white women right before the ears of the men.

I slipped in Harry Belafonte whenever I could, since he didn't sound black and since I really liked his voice.

It was a good thing listeners couldn't see the album covers. Once at WNPT I was on the air as announcer during the Sunday morning Rainbow Quartet segment. The Rainbow Quartet was on WNPT for many years and consisted of a group of white men who sang gospel songs and pitched products and services of whatever sponsors they could come up with. There were many family members and friends who accompanied the Rainbow Quartet when they came to the station and it was always one big party until they left.

One of the quartet members spotted a Count Basie album in my control room, as I was pulling records for the night shift. Basie's face filled the cover. The singer looked at the album, then at me in a slow, calculated manner. Then he smiled and said, "One of our ebony friends, eh?"

That's all he said, but it was clear what he was really saying. I had been put on notice not to get too carried away with my black music.

When George Wallace made his stand in the schoolhouse door (actually, the old Foster Auditorium on the University campus), the radio stations in town decided to pool their news reporting so that paranoia and rumormongering would not get out of hand. Of course, since no station in town did much more than rip-and-read news (rip the copy off the wire machine and read it on the air without so much as a rehearsal or an advance read-through), it could also be said that this was the first time an attempt had been made to cover something controversial while it was happening.

It was generally felt that, should World War III happen to Tuscaloosa, the local stations would record a wire-copy version and play it back the next day.

For some reason, I was assigned to cover the actual event. All I did was stand there a few feet away from George Wallace and watch as he and the federal officials rehearsed their roles.

Media people were everywhere. University officials had every rock, loose bottle, and scrap of trash removed from the campus so that no one would throw or be thrown at. The campus was clean for once. All I learned that day is that big events are very simple at the time they happen. Wallace read his lines, the black students got in, and we all went home. The announcers from all the local radio stations thought it was a lot of fun. I was glad to be alive at the end of the day.

One of the reasons I no longer live in Tuscaloosa is that I voted for the first black woman in history to become Miss Labor Day in Tuscaloosa County.

I was news director of WCFT-TV in Tuscaloosa and went out to cover the Miss Labor Day contest, an annual affair for rednecks and community people and even for black laborers and their families. I had also been invited to be one of the judges for the Miss Labor Day contest. Media people get to judge a lot of beauty contests. Since it was a holiday, thus a slow news day, I decided to cover the contest results after judging the event.

As soon as the contestants started coming onto the stage, it was apparent that one particular dark-skinned girl was the beauty of the day. Several traditional blondes and local creatures looked great, but this one was special. She must be Mexican or Puerto Rican, I figured, since her skin was on the light side of brown. I was wrong, of course, and didn't fully realize it until the vote was almost in. The girl was the daughter of a black labor leader, and the judges were nervous.

"You know we ought to make her runner-up," said one of the judges. "Nobody would mind that," said another. I didn't catch on until later, so I simply said, "She's the prettiest, isn't she?" Everybody agreed and most voted for the girl.

The crowd nearly passed out as one body when the announcement was made. Governor Albert Brewer was on the speaker's platform and turned a bit white. He seemed to disappear soon thereafter. One white woman came over to my mother after the contest and let her have it for having a son who would vote for a black woman. My mother let her have it right back. She seemed pleased at what I had done. The mother of the blonde white runner-up was humiliated because it was impossible for any black woman to be beautiful compared to any white woman. My wife got obscene phone calls from Klan-mentality white males.

Back at the station the next day, Clarence Vogel, the station manager, spent nearly an hour reaming me for being a judge in the contest. He threatened to fire me but never did.

By then, the calls at home were pretty rough. I imagined nightriders coming by the largely glass-walled apartment we lived in and firing into the window.

"I want the shotgun. Where's the shotgun?" I asked my mother, in front of my young and wide-eyed brother and sister. I had gone home to get protection in case anybody threatened me and my wife.

Mother was scared but didn't stand in the way. I got the double-barreled shotgun my father had given me as a boy, a box of shells and stormed out of the house.

Nothing dramatic happened with the gun, fortunately. It just helped me seem stronger than I was.

At the Stafford Hotel barber shop one day, I was getting my hair cut when I realized that Bobby Shelton, Imperial Wizard of the United Klans of America, was sitting next to me getting his hair cut. I had interviewed him a number of times over the years but had not seen him since the Miss Labor Day pageant.

"How's your wife?" Bobby said slowly, not looking at me.

The Klan calls kept racing through my mind. I was angry. But I was scared, too. I just wanted to be left alone.

"She's just fine, Bobby!" I over-emoted. I tried to make a joke. But Bobby just sat silently and said no more.

"Who let a Nigger get into the contest in the first place?" one of the city police officers said loudly to his buddy. They were sitting

across the aisle from me at City Hall, just before a City Council
meeting was to begin. I covered the council meetings and knew the
officers were talking about last week's big event on Labor Day. They
laughed and joked just loudly enough for me to hear them.

The time I covered Stokely Carmichael's first speech in Tuscaloosa was the first time I heard and understood the terms "black
power" and "black is beautiful." The racist lessons I had been
learning from White Tuscaloosa were as powerful as the racist
lessons I learned from Black Tuscaloosa.

"You can't bring cameras in here," the enormous black bodyguard of Stokely Carmichael told me. Since I was only one of a
handful of white people in the auditorium at all-black Stillman
College, and since the auditorium was filled with blacks, I didn't
argue. I was loaded down with a Bolex movie camera, a Nikon 35-
millimeter camera and a lot of film. I didn't know what to do. "You
can go ahead and bring it in, but don't use it," the bodyguard
warned.

It didn't make any sense at the time. The only coverage that
Carmichael was getting in the white press would come from those
of us who were present, and it was obvious from his promotional
techniques that he wanted all the publicity he could get. But he
didn't want white publicity. Only black people were allowed to take
pictures during his speech. The president of the college wouldn't
help out. He looked terrified and cowed by the enormous crowd
and the loud, brutish techniques being used by Carmichael and his
followers to demonstrate black power. We had to settle for a
snapshot on the sly, which we all shared and put on TV the next
night.

"Kill the honkies, kill the honkies!" The wooden floor of the
First African Baptist Church of Tuscaloosa creaked as a nervous,
upset and angry congregation of black people moved around and
talked back to the speakers at the pulpit. It was the night after the
assassination of Martin Luther King, Jr. (Few Southerners would
dignify King by calling him "doctor," since it was widely rumored
that his was an honorary doctorate — no black people knew
enough to get a real degree.) I was not assigned to cover Dr. King's
memorial service, but I always covered stories like this. It was a way
to show my concern for the cause without getting in trouble with
my bosses for any liberal views.

The church contained just three white people, but I somehow

felt safe inside the structure. The honkies the congregation wanted to kill were outside. As a mass they could be hated. It was hard to apply media hatred toward an individual who was sitting next to you in church.

I left church soon, more afraid of cruising rednecks and Klanners than of any black person. My knowledge of civil strife and black and white attitudes was extensive enough now. As a child, I learned to hold my breath when a black person passed me on the bus, headed for the rear ("Colored to rear, white to front"), since black people were supposed to smell bad. I learned not to be sexually attracted to black women, only to media beauties with blonde hair and large breasts and white skin. I watched with fascination as black men began to look at white women in the presence of white men. When I was a child, no black man dared to look with interest at a white woman. I would see an attractive white woman walk by and quickly check out how other men were reacting to her. Whites were always looking. Blacks never looked. Even as a child I didn't buy that. Black men were always caught not looking. It was too studied. They simply didn't dare look. Now they do.

I left Tuscaloosa because I had to get away from people who would never forget my silent anti-racism. Activists were tolerated. Quiet liberals were feared. And we could always be spotted by any redneck. Simply because we did not laugh readily at the racist joke (we didn't criticize, either). We did not cluck and worry along with others about how Niggers were making the world go to Hell. We did not join in. We did not speak.

My children have never seen dual water fountains, segregated buses, black people standing in back of diners at Woolworth's, maids entering through the back door, or black women who could never be called ladies.

But I still hear the slurs and the jokes, and I still have trouble laughing.

HENRIETTA MacGUIRE

è è è

Birmingham, Alabama

I hated the Birmingham of my early days. At night the steel mills flared brilliantly, searing flames from a row of open-hearth furnaces visible from the top of Red Mountain. By day the unarmed workers were gunned down by the National Guard for daring to strike for better pay and more tolerable working conditions. Those were the bitter days of the Depression when Roosevelt was telling the country that one third of our people were "badly fed, badly clothed, and badly housed." Those were the days of total segregation, almost unchanged from the Civil War. Blacks, both urban and rural, lived in unrelieved poverty, with constant humiliations binding them down on every side. Water fountains and rest rooms were designated by COLORED and WHITE, passenger elevators in public buildings were reserved for WHITES ONLY, with blacks forced to use the freight lifts. Trains, buses, waiting rooms, restaurants, theaters and hotels had all had impenetrable barriers designed to keep the races apart. Gangs of black convicts, often chained together in their black-and-white striped clothes, were hired out to white employers to work for a few cents an hour. For the majority of black Americans, in Birmingham, and almost everywhere else, life fitted David Hume's description, "nasty, brutish, and short."

But growing up on the south side of Alabama's largest city, I was only aware of these social forces in a peripheral way. There were other things I hated more. Like being poor. Mine was the quintessential WASP family: father an engineer while mother stayed at home with the children, all of whom had blue eyes, light brown hair, and even white teeth. By hard work and self-sacrifice my father had made a considerable amount of money, but by the time I came along, most of it had been swallowed up by the Depression, and he retained little more than the manners and attitudes of the well-to-do. And a limited number of the trappings: Crown Derby china, cut glass goblets, and an incomplete collection of old family silver. But all the rest was gone. And as time passed, with the Depression worsening and five children in the family, even enough food eventually became a problem. My memory of those years is of carrying home bags of groceries in my arms (the cars had long since been sold), groceries of the cheapest, marked-down prices. Peanut butter was a constant, with homemade apple sauce and cans of sardines often providing the main dishes for a meal. Clothes were always hand-me-downs. They were passed around in the family and worn until they literally fell apart. Skirts were turned up or let down, sweaters had patches on the elbows, and winter coats were filtered down from child to child. My youngest sister somewhat dramatically reports that she got her first new dress the day she went off to college — after the family fortunes had improved.

I hated the limitations that poverty imposed. It didn't help at all that nearly everybody else was poor, too. I found it humiliating to have been forced to move from our lovely, big house on Maplewood Avenue, just off Arlington, from the house with leaded glass doors and a large butler's pantry, to the smaller and less elegant place on South Eighteenth Street. (Even the new address was odious!) It was somehow insulting of fate not to fulfill my unrealistic expectations, vague and confused as they were, about what kind of life I longed for. Like most teenagers, I didn't know what I wanted but I certainly did want it. I only knew that extricating myself from Birmingham was the first step toward a more exciting existence.

High on my Hate List also stood the church, for mine was a devotedly religious family. The First Presbyterian Church downtown on Fourth Avenue North was ours, and it formed the center of my parents' lives. Sundays had about them a military routine: Sunday School at nine-thirty, church at eleven, home for dinner, back downtown at five-forty-five for Young People's Meeting. My father believed in a strict and literal interpretation of the Bible:

God had created the world in six days, and Moses returned from the mountaintop carrying the stone tablets inscribed with the Ten Commandments. Above all, my father remembered the Sabbath Day to keep it holy. And he took care that we did too. No games, no loud talking, no movies, no swimming, no reading anything except the Bible and The Christian Observer. The Observer was a weekly journal published under the direction of the church and it was considered righteous enough for Sunday perusal, for its articles were worthy of the magazine's name. Our one wild fling was to make chocolate fudge on Sunday afternoon, without nuts, because they were too expensive. How we lusted after that fudge!

However, by the time I was a Junior at Ramsey High School, I had begun to draw away from the religious overdoses my family endured. No open withdrawals, because I was too much of a coward to confront my father head-on. But after Sunday School I would slip away from the church grounds and go to a drug store on a nearby corner. There, with my church collection money, I would buy a coke and sometimes a pack of cigarettes — of which my father also disapproved. And I would sit out the sermon huffing and puffing away, and then turn up at the church door to congratulate the minister on an excellent interpretation of the Bible.

But during all those years I was too cowardly to admit what the real problem was: religion, as it was presented by the Presbyterian Church of that period, bored me to death with its repetitiveness. The same Biblical stories endlessly repeated, the same ideas given the same interpretations, the same moral values drummed tirelessly into our heads with no room for questioning or doubt. And even worse, the whole business seemed intellectually insulting. But in addition, on Sundays, to have to swallow the Virgin Birth, the Blind Man regaining his sight, and the water turning into wine — all of that was too much. I rejected the whole thing, though outwardly still going through the motions and despising myself for being so lily-livered.

If it hadn't been for my mother, life in Birmingham would indeed have been deadly. But she was indomitable of spirit and merry of heart, and nothing could defeat her. To every situation she brought a rollicking sense of humor and an ability to perceive the ridiculous. She would read the society page of the newspaper in a flutey, falsetto voice making fun of everything, especially of the reports of weddings in which the bride always came from a "fine, old southern family." My mother would point out that the entire lower half of the United States seemed peopled wall to wall with fine old southern families who did nothing but preserve their grandmother's fine, old lace wedding gown. Or she would attach a rusty safety pin to her chest and announce that she had just been pledged to the most exclusive sorority of all, the Gamma Flamma Goos.

Her family was exceptional because most of its members were widely traveled and spoke several languages. She herself had lived in Europe, had spent a year in Jerusalem while it was still under the Turks, and then had taught English in Puerto Rico during the early days of this century. Several of her relatives still lived outside the United States. Unlike anyone else on our block or even anyone else we knew, we regularly received letters with strange, foreign stamps and exotic postmarks, bringing news of aunts and uncles in Latin America and of a cousin in Japan. One of these uncles returned for a visit after twenty-five years in Brazil. We children were fascinated by his looks for he had become what we considered a typical Brazilian: face darkly tanned from the tropical sun, heavy, clipped mustache when everyone else in Alabama was clean shaven, clothes with a subtle, alien cut. I delighted in his strangeness for it seemed to me a good omen: I interpreted it to mean that I myself would somehow escape from Birmingham and never return.

I eventually did escape but not until after college. At that time Birmingham-Southern was a Methodist school designed to turn out southern ladies and gentlemen who would never question the values of "the southern way of life." We all attended chapel every morning and listened to an inspirational talk about becoming "flowers of southern womanhood." Then we went to classes wearing saddle shoes and white knee socks and straight, narrow skirts which reached halfway down to our ankles. To make it into a sorority was the essence of success. But a sustained interest in ideas or concepts, or intellectual excellence of any kind, was never pursued. No girl in the school (we never referred to ourselves as women) seriously considered preparing herself for a career. We rarely thought about independence and certainly not of a life of one's own. Rather, we marched in lock step from high school to college to the altar and on to diaper rash and the latest formulas for bottle-fed babies.

Middle class girls at that time belonged first to their parents, and then to their husbands and children, and nowhere along the road was there a way station for themselves. Looking back on those days after so much time and travel I am struck by several things. First of all, there was a curious kind of innocence about our lives that is almost inconceivable in today's world. The child in elementary school in the 1980s seems to me less protected and better informed about life than I was as a sophomore in college. I had never heard of homosexuality or oral sex, and drugs were simply unimaginable. Our values were largely those of Hollywood's higher morality: the poor and honest young man always triumphed and the wicked were smitten hip and thigh. The world of "J.R." and "Dynasty" would have seemed so foreign they would have been treated as high comedy. Second, growing up in Alabama in the '30s and '40s, we were surrounded by taboos; taboos regarding language, behavior, sex, work, race, and ideas. In as rigidly structured a family as mine, deviating from the accepted code not only would never have been permitted, it would not even have occurred to us. And third, I feel that the narrow straitjacket of our world produced those two kinds of people society is always divided into: those who accepted most of the mores and morals and somehow accommodated themselves, or else those, like me, who rejected much of our backgrounds and got out.

After an absence of twenty years in New York, Costa Rica, and various countries of Europe, I'm glad to be back in Alabama — some of the time. The unfailing good manners still impress me. For the middle class, life has a gentleness you don't find in many other places. And most of all, people here still have time. It requires large amounts of time to cultivate friendship, to nurture it with care, cherishing and protecting it through fat years and lean. That was perhaps the most significant lesson Alabama taught me: to be willing to make the necessary commitments of time to nourish the human spirit.

MARIE STOKES JEMISON

Montgomery, Alabama

There were six horses on my grandmother's porch the night I was born. A stable close to town burned and the horses were freed to wander. My grandmother lived on lower Court Street, not far from the stable. It was said that my father beat the horses off with a broom to allow the doctor to enter.

None of this excitement was said to phase my grandmother, who calmly continued the nightly game of hearts she played with her sister-in-law in the dining room.

My grandfather had gone to an early alcoholic grave, but his three sisters and their three husbands lived together in the family home at 502 Perry Street. This family commune adored my mother who did not get along with her own high-spirited mother, who made her living running a boarding house for young men who came to Montgomery to work. Mother had lived in the commune since she was a child, but had agreed to have this first grandchild at her mother's as offset to the recent accidental death of her only brother, Wade Hampton Hannon, at sixteen. The mother and two daughters were heartbroken.

On this cold December night, my mother's three aunts and three uncles crouched beneath the window of the front bedroom where my mother labored. It was 2:30 a.m. when I bawled into the world. My father raised the window. "It's a girl."

I grew to feel that beside my regular grandmother, I had three others. My father, who was from Ozark, had very little family, and there were no grandparents there. But I had the three great uncles. All this crowd doted on my mother and she returned the affection.

My early childhood was spent in a little house on Sayre Street and every day great uncle Henry Mourning, married to Tattie (Caroline), came to take me to ride. Heinie, as I called him, came from the Kentucky mountains. Occasionally, his mother, a mountain school teacher, whom we called Mother Mourning, came to visit. She was a tiny, frail little old lady wearing a long white dress and a little cap. Years later when John Kennedy was inaugurated, John Sherman Cooper, Senator from Kentucky, secured a ticket for me on the reviewing stand in memory of Mother Mourning who taught him in those Cumberland mountains.

Mother and one of her friends drove to town every day to go to the bank. I was always on the back seat and usually on the way going or coming we stopped at 502 Perry to rock on the porch and drink Coca Cola with the great aunts and their friends. Perry Street was the main social street in Montgomery, and the Perry Street house was a gathering place because of the number of people in residence.

I loved sitting among all those women, with their gaily painted faces, listening to their funny stories and gossip. They treated me seriously, as if I were one of them. I was never made to feel a nuisance or unwanted. Sometimes we went straight to the bank and afterwards double parked at Harry's Soda Fountain across the street from the bank. Mother and her friend ordered "Dopes" and I had a cherry smash. When the car hop fastened the tray to the window, there were two fountain cokes in glasses and a tiny paper cup beside them. Mother would lift the two aspirins from the cup and plop one in each coke. It took me awhile to understand that the caffeine in the coke combined with the aspirin gave the girls a small high.

In winter mother would go to New York for several months to shop and see the theater. The aunts' dear friend, Georgia Oates, also went to New York in winter. Her daughter, Marion, my friend, and I went to Perry Street to spend that time. By this time we were in school so Bolling, the chauffeur for the household, drove us to school from there. In the early morning he would tip-toe in and light the fire. Then the march began. The women in their frilly negligees and the men in robes would gather around our big four poster bed. Bolling then brought in breakfast trays and Marion and

I held court until it was time to dress. I always had much to say and my mother's friends began to call me "Who-Mamma? Who?"

The aunts and uncles listened patiently and attentively to all our questions and conversation and tried to answer honestly. At night they put on costumes from the trunk under the stair, told us stories and put on plays for us. Marion and I loved this time every winter. It's no wonder, for this household revolved around the pleasure and well-being of two small girls.

Marion's own house was fascinating to visit. Georgia and Will Oates and Georgia's mother, Mimi Saffold, along with Marion, lived in a 1929 version of Tara. It was called "Belvoir" after the Mississippi plantation of Jefferson Davis. Georgia, a stickler for authenticity, imported gray moss to decorate the trees. A small, curly headed blond charmer, Georgia Saffold had been one of the great southern belles of pre-World War I fame. Men were said to go wild for her, throw themselves off bridges, and one was a suicide when she denied him. But she was no dumb blonde. My father who admired her extravagantly said about her: "She may look like a china doll but she thinks like a man." That remark made me furious even then.

The Oates-Saffold household was irresistible for a pubescent kid in that innocent time between world wars and before the bomb. Mimi lay a-bed all day writing negro dialect stories published occasionally in the local paper, but more often she read them at her meetings of the Alabama Pen Women.

In summer, Georgia put a cambric smock over her girdle and a pith helmet over her curls and went to work with Rufus in the garden. All morning they raked, chopped, and hauled. Then coming in she stripped to her girdle before the electric fan to eat a farmhand's lunch of cabbage, black-eyed peas, okra, cornbread and iced tea. While wolfing down this kitchen meal, she told us bawdy tales of growing up southern. As dainty as she appeared to men, to me she was a funny, lively, unselfconscious woman. After dinner, she walked around upstairs in her girdle stopping before one electric fan and then another, and for an hour of the time played her large harp which stood in the parlor. She wore nothing but her girdle. Late in the afternoon, the two women bathed and dressed in long hostess gowns and received men on the veranda.

Georgia wore pastel gowns but Mimi wore black both winter and summer. "For my dear departed Mr. Saffold," she told me. Both women always wore a pink rose in their low decolletage.

Europeans were on the porch in summer. They were usually heel-clicking Germans the women had met on their trips abroad. Marion and I were not encouraged to visit the veranda, so we lay on our stomachs on a small balcony projecting out from Georgia's room upstairs. Rufus, now in a white coat, served Blue Moon cocktails and the ladies fanned themselves and flirted. After we gave the strangers time to catch on, we made it clear we expected chewing gum. The punishment for those who forgot was a rain of spit balls.

Will Oates, dark, tall and romantic-looking, spent no time on the veranda, in fact we saw little of him at all. He worked at some state job. His father, William Oates, had been governor. Will was the only child of the governor and his wife Sarah Toney, but he was not the only child of the governor. There is the tale that once on the campaign trail some heckler called out "Governor what you gonna do about yo yard chillen?" The governor without missing a beat yelled back: "I'm gonna educate mine. What you gonna do about yours?"

It was obvious to me even so young that it was the Saffold women who counted, who had imagination and get-up-and-go. Not poor Will. I was always conscious that my beautiful, dark-haired, hazel-eyed mother was attractive to men and that she liked them also. When I couldn't have been over five I think I got my first inkling about sexual attraction. Mother met Mr. Richardson on the steamer that used to run between Savannah and New York. He was president of the steamship line. The next spring Mr. Richardson arrived in Montgomery on his private railway car. For some reason Mother took me with her to have supper on his car parked in the Union Station. I remember looking at my mother objectively, if five-year-old eyes could do that, when I saw the look in Mr. Richardson's eye as we entered the car. She wore a filmy peach dress with peach feathers around the hem. Her shoulders were bare, covered only with tiny rhinestone straps and she smelled of roses. Mr. Richardson, a tall slender man with a small mustache, greeted me warmly, never taking his eye off my mother. A white-coated butler brought out movie books, a Coca Cola and a Hershey Bar. This suitable entertainment was not near as diverting as what my child's eyes saw that night. I saw a grown man smitten and I felt an alien and unfamiliar pain. I was too young to identify my feelings but they were different. Somebody else, a stranger, was competing for her attention and getting it. Mr. Richardson sent us home in his car. On the way I asked: "Mother, does Daddy like Mr. Richardson as much as you do?" She looked over at me on the backseat with her finger to her lips: "Sh, Sh," she advised me. "We don't want to talk in front of the chauffeur about private business." I never was taken to see Mr. Richardson again.

ROSE M. SANDERS

❧ ❧ ❧

Mobile, Alabama

S he ruled the whole wide world. At the time I harbored these thoughts of my Grandmother Mitchel, my knowledge of the world was as limited as my travels, vicarious and otherwise. But I was more fortunate than most of my peers. My father, by the dictates of his profession and religious association, was required to move from city to city and state to state throughout the Southland, to save "colored souls." His mission to spread the gospel by no means excluded his white brothering and sistering, but they apparently deemed it necessary to exclude themselves. Reb — Daddy, that is — was always ready to accept another church, another city, another challenge. And Mama was always willing to follow him. God never made a better preacher's wife than my mama. Lord knows He couldn't make a better mama. Of course she was just a chip off the old block. She was my grandmother's daughter.

During my early childhood, we were truly a family on the move. New faces and old faces darted in and out or our lives. Whenever the day to depart our newest home arrived, the family was always choked with emotions but our pioneer spirit always overcame our desire to remain.

The one stable place in our lives that we could always call home was Alabama. The things that made it good are seemingly paradoxical, because at the time of my experience, many of those things were considered by me, my siblings, and my cousins to be nothing less than bad.

Grandma Mitchel was at the centerpoint of those experiences, or it may be more correct to say that she was their architect. Mama

Mitchel, which is what we usually called her, moved from Wilcox County in her youth and stationed herself permanently in Mobile County. That is, her physical being was in Mobile County. As far as I was concerned, Grandma Mitchel was everywhere. I must have moved in and out of six different towns from the time of my birth to my seventh birthday, but there was one place to which I always returned: Grandma Mitchel's house in Mobile County. Between each "return" I could hear her talking to me. "Have you said your prayers, gal?" Seemed like that voice would come from nowhere when I, alone and unseen, would decide that the Lord didn't need to hear from me that day. I would skeptically check out the room just to make sure that no one was in the room but me. I never saw anybody but I knew she was there. She talked about God so much that sometimes I thought she was something between an angel and a saint, not that I knew the difference between the two. I never thought of her as a preacher, though. Never saw a woman preacher in those days. Funny, it was easier to fantasize about her being an angel than to grasp the possibility that she could be one of those ministers called by God himself to preach the gospel.

I used to hear a lot of my daddy's friends talk about how they had been called by God to save souls. Usually, the call came when they were on some lonely road near the brink of irreversible damnation. The voice was always male. My father had a peculiar way of avoiding this subject. I never heard him tell one of the miracle stories, but he was a man who practiced what he preached, unlike many of his colleagues who had been "miraculously" called to preach. They often found it unnecessary to practice their religion. To preach it was sufficient.

Grandma Mitchel loved preachers, especially her own. But that was man's work. I truly believe she wanted to be a minister. She never said that, but in retrospect it seems that a lot of her push and drive was channeled to her grandchildren to compensate for dreams unfulfilled. She was smart as a whip. You couldn't hide anything from her, and she could bore a hole in a lie quicker than a drill could bore a hole in paperwood. I heard so much about right and wrong during my formative years that I grieved when I thought about doing something bad. And when I actually did wrong I got punished twice, once by Grandma and then by my guilt-stricken conscience. Always made me feel good though, to hear her say,

"You gonna be somebody, gal. Lord done already worked it out. Just keep your eye on your dreams and hold on."

As far as I was concerned, Grandmother was more than a preacher, she was almost an angel. Sometimes, though, she would get to preaching to us so hard about good and bad and all that in between that I would conclude, and say to myself, "She ain't no angel. She just want us to be one. Anyway," I'd say, "the way she swing a switch, she must be some kin to the devil. She sho 'mean' enough to be his cousin." I would feel real bad for thinking such thoughts as soon as my anger subsided.

Seems like the older we got, the tougher she got. Granddaddy was strong and firm, but he made it clear that when it came to discipline on the yard, Grandma reigned supreme. At some point in our lives, over 20 cousins stayed in the yard under her reign. She ruled over my life in and out of Alabama, then and for years to come.

She kept me and my older and younger brothers one full year during our early childhood. We lived in the heart of the black Mobile community in an old but well-kept white house. Behind the house stood a smaller wood house which was built to shelter my aunt and uncle and their host of children. Before I formally learned about Africa and the extended family concept, I was a direct beneficiary of this precious relic of African culture that had managed to survive the Civil War, and all wars thereafter.

Both houses were surrounded by a fence. At the time, that fence seemed to be the tallest fence in the whole world. Beyond that fence, that year in Mobile is a real blank in my life. Mobile was a mystery. I never saw the majestic waters that brushed the skirt-tail of the city. Nor did I see the busy city people darting about their urban lives. If I saw a glimmer of these things I blanked them all out. My remembrance of Mobile is confined to that tall, tall fence that separated the yard from the rest of the world. When my parents came to retrieve us from our Mobile world, we stared in bewilderment at the somewhat familiar strangers who had come to take us away. I later learned that Papa and Mama were distressed by our apparent childhood amnesia and vowed never to leave us again for a substantial period of time. They never did.

My most vivid memories of my life in Alabama were of subsequent summers spent with Grandma Mitchel in the yard, as we came to call our Alabama homeplace. We were confined to the yard except to attend church. Occasionally, at my father's insistence, we would venture briefly onto Davis Avenue. There I saw my first swimming pool. Black people seemed to own the whole town. They were everywhere.

"Too much evil in the world," Grandma Mitchel would respond to most of our requests to leave the yard. So after awhile, I and my host of cousins pretended to accept our fate. But the yearning to venture beyond the yard remained strong. So we fantasized. Many days were spent creating plays and skits that we acted out as seriously as Broadway's best. Very little was reduced to writing, but the make believe worlds we created gave us a sense of freedom that transcended that tall fence and the "evil" beyond its bounds. Much of my compassion for life was born in the yard. I was sheltered from many realities, the painful and the joyous ones. The dynamics of my captivity were not understood by me at the time.

In later years, I came to understand that I was being sheltered from a more harsh and painful captivity. That old lady was a hell of a woman. She represented all the pain and joy that the women of her era had experienced. Dreams deemed unattainable were placed on hold and quietly transferred to the next generation. When it became clear that many of the dreams could not be reached by the next generation, they were placed on hold and quietly transferred to the next.

What we perceived as Grandma Mitchel's meanness was really fear. Fear that the dream could not be achieved. Fear that the obstacles could not be overcome. Fear that the "evil" beyond the yard would consume us and extinguish the desire to dream.

The years passed slowly and uneventfully. My family moved from one small southern town to the other. Every year we returned to the yard in Mobile, Alabama.

In the spring of 1963, I completed my freshman year of college at a small black college in urban North Carolina that was also surrounded by a tall invisible fence. The university yard, just as Grandma Mitchel's yard, stood high and forbade me to venture beyond its protective bounds. Both yards had held me captive from the harsh realities of southern and modern life.

During my freshman year, my parents again heeded the call of the ministry. We moved into a big white house on the notorious

Dynamite Hill in Birmingham, Alabama. The neighborhood painfully earned that name because of the numerous bombings its residents had experienced.

During the late spring of that year I turned 18. Most of my life had been sheltered by a fence, visible and invisible. That fence came tumbling down in the summer of 1963.

It was a nightmare far greater than my mind had ever conceived in slumber. The sound of frantic screams pushed us up from the dinner table and out to the streets of Dynamite Hill. People poured from their homes, going nowhere. The home is supposed to be a place of refuge in the time of storm. But diabolic intruders had come and literally shook the very foundation of the homes on Dynamite Hill. More importantly, they shook and reshaped the lives of those who dwelled therein. The intruders came uninvited, clothed with the appearance of respectability. They came in blue. They came to continue or to revive the unfinished Civil War. They came to kill. They were law men.

My parents summoned us back into the house but we were overwhelmed by the clamor of hurried feet and voices filled with fright and wonder. The magnetism of the situation pulled me beyond the yard and over that tall fence that still stood invisibly before me. I was swept into the sea of human flesh, moving toward the slaughter. A house near the top of Dynamite Hill had been bombed again. No one felt safe in their homes nor on the street and so the crowd moved frantically and unknowingly. Suddenly, out of the darkness, from the direction of the men in blue, came a flurry of bullets. One rested in the body of a young black man. When he fell to the ground, the crowd scattered in hushed anger and pronounced fear. The young man was left dying in the street. A few loyal kinsmen or friends, delayed temporarily by fear, suddenly ended their retreat, rushed to him, knelt and wept. I never knew his name. I didn't read the paper or inquire. I wanted to forget the nightmare and seek the refuge of the yard and that tall, tall fence which forbade evil to enter, or forbade me to exit to places where evil resided. But in the summer of 1963, that tall, tall fence came tumbling down and I knew that it could never be rebuilt.

The one thing that held it all together was Grandma Mitchel's prodding me to achieve the dream. I had to be strong and good to achieve it. Grandma Mitchel knew this all along. For the first time I began to understand the obstacles that dared me to even try. But it was too late for me to fail. I no longer needed the protection of the yard or that tall, tall fence. The legacy of strength and determination had been firmly planted by Grandma Mitchel and nurtured and watered by my parents.

I finished college number one in my class, and journeyed on to law school, but I knew the dream had not been achieved. I had to leave Alabama to attend law school because no law school in the state admitted blacks in the mid-sixties. I finished Harvard University, a so-called top rated law school, but the dream remained unachieved. I grew to understand that the dream wouldn't be achieved until all the folks in the yard achieved it. That's what Grandma Mitchel's yard was all about. In her own way she was trying to make sure that everybody in the yard achieved the dream.

MARTIN HAMES

Birmingham, Alabama

Life in the West End of Birmingham, Alabama, was blissful for those of us growing up there, born in the Depression and facing pubescence and maturity in the 1950s. I remember it more fondly as the years pass. Among the most exciting things about it were softball, the movies, and our gang from Stonewall Jackson Elementary School.

We spent many evening hours every week all summer long at the softball field behind the watermelon stand behind the fire station near the Seventh Day Adventist Church. Every organization, every business of any size in the community fielded a team. It was almost impossible to be partisan as one had friends or relatives on any number of teams. Frequently the Tri-Hy-Y at West End High sold refreshments.

By far the best of all the players was Lena Robertson. She was a pitcher and sported the best underhand in southern softball. There was not one feminine aspect to her persona but she was friendly and we liked her. Every Tuesday and Friday night of the summer season, her sisters and her father came out to watch her pitch.

Mrs. Doris Robertson, Lena's mother, was a close friend of my grandmother. Mrs. Robertson wore sheer dresses and hats with plumes on them. She and Nannie wrote a masterly cookbook and sold it for the benefit of the Thelma Norton Circle. It was so good that it went into two printings and is still in use in my household today. It brought in several hundred dollars for the Leper Fund. Mrs. Robertson sang in the choir — a little off-key. She also hand-decorated lingerie for all the young brides' trousseaus. All in all she was too busy to watch anything — even softball.

Between 1945 and 1950, my friend Lula Belle and I organized the West End Movie Review Club. It was dedicated "with undying love to Tallulah Bankhead, Clark Gable, and Brother J. W. McBrayer." The least famous of the three aforenamed was the minister at Beverly Methodist Church who had caught our fancy. This club usually gathered in front of the Crauswells' house and hiked to Alley's Drugstore on Tuscaloosa Avenue. There we indulged ourselves in homemade fried pies and egg salad sandwiches on white toast.

After Mother's dear friend, Glaze, opened the hamburger stand left vacant by the robbery-murder of Mr. Goatlet, the former owner, we deserted Alley's and stopped to eat with Aunt Glaze. Hamburgers were a quarter, homemade chocolate pies fifteen cents, and cokes a nickel. One could enjoy a delicious lunch for fifty cents — a sinful indulgence for seventy-five!

Then into the movies. This cost a dime and every Saturday it included a weekly serial and a double feature with newsreels, previews, and cartoons. Our favorite summer season serial ran in 1948: Superman vs. Spider Woman in eighteen installments. It was a weekly exercise in raw emotion. The stars of our day were Gene Autry, Lash LaRue, Andy Devine, Monte Hale, Al "Fuzzy" St. John, Gabby Hayes, The Riders of the Purple Sage, and of course, Roy Rogers, Dale, and Trigger. We died over Gordon McRae and Doris Day in Moonlight Bay. Liz Taylor, Margaret O'Brien, June Allyson, et al. in Little Women sent us scurrying to the bathroom, so we didn't have to admit that Beth's death had made us cry. Most of these "biggies" were shown in downtown Birmingham.

At least once a month we got "let-off" downtown to do the movie scene. The rules were simple. Be at the appointed place to go home and never go to the bathroom in the Alabama Theatre alone as there were three or four "queers" in Birmingham and that's where they "hang out."

On those days we ate at the Corner Soda for luncheon. The menu there was standard: a boiled bean bun with mustard and a coke. This lunch was 36 cents. We started the day at the Galax at 10:45 a.m., then proceeded to the Strand or the Newmar. We felt something special for the Strand because that utterly racist document, "Song of the South," played there for 108 weeks. We knew the script word for word before it finally departed. Could that have been our answer to "Rocky Horror?"

After lunch, we hit the Empire or the Melba, the Alabama or the Ritz. We would get picked up at 7:00 or 7:30 p.m. and rushed away to dinner. We only went to the Lyric to throw maraschino cherries from the balcony.

When we went to town with our mothers, we ate at the Twentieth Street Britlings. We always had crab cutlets and hot slaw. This we did with gusto because Mrs. Slaughter, the hostess, was another one of our idols. She was tall, dark, bejeweled, mysterious — in the Signe Hasso, Benay Venuta tradition. We nominated her for six straight years for the BPW Woman of the Year Award.

Our group, led by the dauntless Lula Belle, assured the community of periodic excitement. Inspired by the Man-Eater of Koamon, we dug a deep hole in a nearby field and covered it with branches. The girl we ran into the hole was thought lost and the police searched for her all day. Oh well, someone had to be the tiger. Another time, inspired by Tarzan, we "branded" an outcast from another section of West End because he wouldn't reveal the location of the elephant's graveyard.

We did everything together, from collecting papers for the weekly drive at Stonewall Jackson Elementary School to preparing Easter Sunrise service at the Slag Pits at Spaulding Mines. We separated to sell savings stamps and war bonds, for the weekly winner got a free ride on a Sherman tank. Funny, in those days we hated war just as much as we do now, but it made us love instead of, as it seems to do today, hate each other.

One year for Easter Sunrise service we set up an altar near the Slag Pits at the Spaulding Mines. We planned a glorious celebration of the Resurrection; as it turned out, it was less glorious but more memorable than most. When we arrived at the site, we gathered our hands in a chain of love and began to march up the hill toward the makeshift altar of concrete blocks, sheets, and juice cans wrapped in florist foil and filled with gladioli from the Harbor Hills Glad Farm. We sang, and our song almost filled the morning . . .

"On a hill far-away,"
"Geez, what's that singing?"
"Stood an old rugged cross."

"We got to get the hell outa' here."

"The emblem of suff'ring and shame ..."

"What about all this booze?"

"And I'll love that old cross ..."

"Screw it, boys, let's move!"

"Till my trophies at last I lay down ..."

"That's bootleggers!" shouted Lula Belle.

"I'll cherish the old rugged cross ..."

A truck roared off into the morning, leaving behind the mixture of exhaust fumes and moonshine.

"And exchange it some day for a crown."

SUE WALKER

è è è

Mobile, Alabama

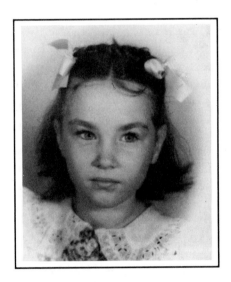

I know that Georgia House remembers. Remembers with absolute fidelity the years from 1946 to 1957 when I was part of its family, for it owned us as much as we owned it — that domed old house on Georgia Street. And though someone else inhabits its kitchen, its parlors and halls, it misses Grandma's limp as she hurries around her high canopy bed fluffing up the eiderdown. It misses the smell of her pork roast baking in the oven, and the avocado sprouting in a mason jar on her screened back porch.

Often when I drive to town, I pass by Georgia House to tell it how well it has held up since Grandma passed away, and how sorry I am that it was sold on the market — sold with my memories and dreams. I tell it yellow isn't its best color at all. It should be white again — with awnings striped blue, hanging like a bonnet over the face of the porch that spread right in a lopsided grin.

I realize that it holds more secrets than even I shall ever know. Whoever sleeps in the middle bedroom now will never know how Grandma died there, with a letter from me tucked beneath the pillow that held her head. Dad said she lay there all peaceful, then suddenly looked up and cried: "Well, hello Webster," held out her hands to receive her husband again, and closed her eyes. A house holds both living and dying dear, harbors them warm in wooden walls.

The back room was where I always stayed — with the largest single closet I have ever known. Even new houses with walk-ins can't boast of a closet so grand — a closet long enough to practice a *pas de bouree* in and dream its four walls were a dressing room for a star performing in Paris or Rome. Grandpa kept his safe in there — a big iron monster that lured a child to spin its silver dials and watch them flash, hear the click click that accompanied in staccato beat. And we would venture in there, Grandpa and I, where he would pull up a cane-backed chair, sit me on his lap, and instruct me in the intricacies of knobbery. These numbers became our special secret, and I would have gladly let a robber slit my throat before I told that combination. It belonged to Grandpa and to me.

But nowhere were there more happy hours to hold than in the kitchen where Grandma rolled out dumpling dough on the marble-topped table by the wall. It was the place I could stick my fingers into dough, feel the stretch of it, and flour myself up to my elbows in white. I think I became something of the woman that I am in that kitchen — learning how conversation and love were kneaded together, how they were stirred into turnip greens and tasted in pot liquor. Sharing was special — even washing up without a dishwasher after the meal was done.

All of this Georgia House remembers . . . and I do too. Perhaps that is why I drive by today and talk to it — renewing the memories it houses and holds.

MARIE F. GILLESPIE

🐛 🐛 🐛

Fairfield, Alabama

I was four years old and time stood still. Congeniality was a way of life. Our family was new in Birmingham, having just moved from Lockhart, a small Alabama town near the Florida line. I was heartbroken over leaving Grandma's rambling old house with the two orange trees growing in the front yard. I missed Big Tom, the cat that seemed forever hovering around my feet. A distant move like this was not the best thing in the world that could happen to a little girl. I longed to sit beside Grandma again on the back steps and help her shell peas, freshly gathered from the garden. She was a small lady with dark hair, neatly bunned, that never did turn grey. Grandpa, tall, thin and balding with a droopy mustache, often let me sit on his lap while he told outlandish tales to keep me laughing. He was never very energetic but was lovable even though he liked to drink.

Daddy had found a house to rent in Fairfield not far from the Wire Mill, a part of the Tennessee Coal and Iron Company, commonly referred to as the T.C.I. Living in the shadow of the South's leading iron and steel producing center was a different way of life for us. We soon learned to love and appreciate the orange glow that flashed upward from the blast furnaces painting the sky at night. We listened with anticipation for the blowing of the whistles at noontime and again when the work shifts changed. The furnaces were the source of income for most of the families that we knew.

One day word came that Grandpa was not expected to live. Mama and Daddy had only three girls at that time, Ruth, Lucile, and me. We were taken shopping and outfitted with new coats and caps. The weather was cold when the sad journey by train began. Grandpa was gone when we arrived.

It was not long afterward when Grandma, two uncles, and an aunt decided to move to Birmingham. They settled in Fairfield too and I was happy again. Going to Grandma's house was always a special occasion for me.

I was born in Lockhart and was the oldest of eight eventually — six girls and two boys. My parents were William Mallory and Nora Bell Franklin. Daddy was a carpenter, an expert in his field, although self-taught. The fancy trim on some of Birmingham's older church buildings is a testimony to his expertise. He was part Indian and enjoyed fishing and hunting. Daddy was probably familiar with every river, stream, and branch in the state. I remember fondly an expression of his: "The best sleeping in the world is in the woods under a tree with a rock for a pillow."

Daddy kept hound dogs. There was one in particular that he named "Old Blue." He had a cow horn that he took with him when he and Old Blue went hunting. One long blast from it would always bring the dog to his side after a hunt was over.

Another part of Daddy's hunting equipment was a carbide lamp that he attached to the front of his cap. It made a very bright and far-reaching light. Every so often the carbide needed to be emptied and some fresh put in. A foul, never-to-be forgotten odor filled the air on such occasions.

One cold winter morning Daddy came home with a bobcat that he had killed. He stretched it out across the floor in front of the fireplace to let us marvel at how big it was. Later he took it to Mr. Wren, a friend and owner of Wren's Hardware on Gary Avenue, in the heart of downtown Fairfield. Mr. Wren had it stuffed and mounted and displayed in his store window for a long time.

When Daddy wasn't working he frequently could be found meandering in the woods someplace, with dog and rifle by his side. Many Sunday mornings, upon arising to dress for church, we were greeted by the sight of a skillet full of tender squirrel meat smothered in gravy, accompanied by fluffy hot biscuits.

Across the way from where we lived stood a long brick structure, the T.C.I. apartments. A bluff separated the building from our street. Every spring and summer the bluff was completely covered with little roses. The pale pink petals shimmered with dew as we gathered bouquets in the early part of the day to take home to Mama.

Mama was a home-loving soul who found fulfillment in caring for her home and children. A rocking chair played an important part in our upbringing. Today the old-fashioned rocker is considered more or less an antique and is not put to use much.

Mama became terribly upset when any of us were ill. I vividly recall her patient and enduring efforts when my brother Bill came down with polio just about the time that he was learning to walk. Doctors made house calls then and we were quarantined for several weeks. That meant being confined to the premises and having no visitors. Daddy left the house only for emergencies. A dark brown medicine, called Argyrol, was put into our noses every day with an eyedropper to help diminish our chances of getting the disease. Bill survived but one leg was paralyzed from the hip down and he has always worn a brace.

My sister Jeanette had a bout with erysipelus when she was a baby. Medicated gauze had to be wrapped around her legs and body and changed daily as the malady advanced upward. The doctor warned that if it reached her brain she would die. Fortunately it stopped before it went beyond her neck. Mama was at her bedside night and day. And so it was with all eight of us children through many sicknesses and accidents.

Routeman's was the big dry goods store in Fairfield and Johnny Long's Barber Shop was a favorite of the men. Gandy's Drug Store was a popular place. My Aunt Bessie bought her cosmetics there. The first permanent wave that I remember was the one Aunt Bessie came up with. I believe it was called a Marcel.

A stroke left Grandma blind for the last few years of her life. With her clutching my arm we took many walks together. She had a tendency to lean a little to one side but we coped very well on those outings.

Uncle Hobart, who was a bachelor, was especially attentive to Grandma. He worked at the old post office downtown. Many nights after work he would bring something special home for his mother to eat after she became blind. One time it might be a quart bottle of Welch's Pure Grape Juice; another time a watermelon (in season, of course). He would cut it and wake her up even though it would be around midnight. She loved watermelon. Another of her favorite foods was Concord grapes. At that time they came packed in oval-shaped wooden baskets with a wooden lid and handle. What a delightful aroma escaped when the top was removed!

In my young mind the world did not extend beyond the boundaries of Fairfield. All the pleasures of childhood, simple as they were, centered around our community. All of our friends and neighbors were poor folks. That was fine with me because I knew no other life. Anyway we felt like queens every weekend. Daddy got paid on Friday and when he came home with groceries, nestled among the other items was always a bag of candy. A favorite kind was multi-colored suckers made into the shape of tiny brooms. We swept our tongues until they were livid.

I started school at age six at the old 53rd Street School in Fairfield. It was down the hill from where we lived. My first grade teacher, Mrs. Frank Leslie, was especially kind to me, sensing that I was painfully shy. In school I actually spent more time drawing pictures than I did studying.

By age thirteen I was progressing pretty well with what I hoped would be a novel. I had a great imagination. My English teacher, a Mrs. Davis, was quite interested in my efforts and some days she had me read portions of it to the class.

One day she asked us to put our heads down on our desks and close our eyes. The first one to be able to recite the alphabet backward was to raise his or her hand. I do not think she really expected any response. She apparently wanted a few minutes of quiet time for herself. In my subconscious I took four letters at a time, reciting them over and over until I had memorized the entire alphabet. Then I raised my hand.

"Have you really memorized the alphabet backward?" she asked quizzically.

"I think I can say it," I replied. "Well, let us hear you," she demanded. After the muffled snickering around the room stopped, I began ... "ZYXW — VUTS — RQPO — NMLK — JIHG — FEDC — BA."

Her only comment was, "Well, I have never known but one other person who could recite the ABCs backward and he was a college professor."

I had two close girlfriends throughout my grammar and junior high school years. Anita, Elizabeth, and I were known as "the three stooges." Sometimes we fancied ourselves in love but the objects of our affections never knew. We wrote mushy love notes on scraps of paper, folded them and buried them beneath trees on the vacant lot next to our house. Perhaps we thought the "god of love" would retrieve them and deliver them. I do not remember.

We moved several times over the years and by the time I entered high school we lived at the opposite edge of Fairfield. The street running along one side of our house separated Fairfield and Ensley. We walked past the flag pole each day to the 43rd Street Fairfield High School. The flag pole was a landmark in Fairfield. It stood proudly on a circular grassy plot.

In the fall Daddy frequented the curb market downtown. He would return home after those trips with our T Model Ford loaded down with delectables. Sometimes I got to go with him. What an experience that was! Stall after stall filled with orange pumpkins, mountains of turnip, collard and mustard greens, crates of apples and truckloads of sweet potatoes! Daddy thought that Ribbon Cane syrup was better than sorghum. He bought gallon buckets of it.

But the greatest treat of all was the purple stalks of sugar cane that he never passed up. He would sit patiently before the fire, peeling, splitting and cutting two-inch lengths of the sweet cane. When he was finished, Mama's big dishpan would be heaped to overflowing. We would all have a sugar cane jubilee, chewing each piece until it was dry as a corn shuck. We seemed driven to savor every drop of the delicious juice.

A gathering place of young people was the Ensley park and swimming pool. There was a grandstand where one could sit and look down at the swimmers in the pool. A flight of stairs led you to that enchanting area where a lot of "sparking" took place.

A rare treat was riding into downtown Birmingham on the streetcar. This was before buses made their appearance. The fare was only seven cents and the conductor who strode through the aisle collecting fares looked so important in his tailored uniform. In the winter when the weather was cold the best place to sit was behind the motorman in the side seat. It was so cozy and warm there. In the summer the open windows caught all the cool breezes.

We seemed always to live adjacent to a vacant lot. They were the playgrounds of my generation. Life was good. There was no thought of child molestation, dope addiction was unknown, and drinking was limited more or less to a segment of older men. Overall there was trust and caring for one's fellow man.

During my growing-up years Daddy kept a milk cow. They were permitted in the city then, but only a few people had them. I learned to milk at an early age but never overcame my fear of the cow. I would place my milk stool as far away as possible from the cow. At some point during my milking ventures I became afflicted with St. Vitus Dance, a nerve disorder. Doctor's orders put an end to my milking chores and I was allowed to stay at Grandma's house to recuperate.

We had a yard full of game chickens for eating and laying. It was an inexpressible joy for me to come upon a next of eggs carefully hidden in high weeds. Even more thrilling were the times when baby chicks ran about the backyard, tiny balls of yellow fluff, with an occasional black one in the bunch. I loved throwing grain out for them at feeding time.

I had my first date when I was sixteen. Eddie and I walked to the picture show which was quite a distance from where we lived at that time. He was a neighborhood boy and a perfect gentleman, even though several years older than I. We were not in a hurry to grow up.

Almost everyone had a porch swing. Many dreams for the future were spun while swinging, especially at nighttime.

Long before the "bobby sox" era there was the "Whoopee socks" craze. My first pair of ankle socks were white with bright orange checkered tops that turned down. I thought they were so pretty.

Gospel tent meetings were a frequent attraction in Ensley during my teen years. Sawdust floors, folding chairs, and fire and brimstone preaching added to the allure. A group of us went to every revival that came to town.

One of the most exciting events of the year was the Alabama State Fair. School turned out at one o'clock on Children's Day and we all had free admission. More than likely I didn't have a dime to my name, but I always had a great time walking and looking. I often thought of joining the Fair group when they were getting ready to move on. I was too naive to see beyond the glitter and excitement. Thankfully, a Guiding Hand stayed my course.

Street carnivals were another form of amusement that came to Ensley. They were a little like miniature fairs. Those were magical times, riding on the ferris wheel, swings, and merry-go-round.

The Great Depression wiped out Daddy's small savings when the First National Bank of Ensley closed its doors. But like most people we struggled through that time.

Before nylon stockings made the scene, silk hose could be bought for forty-nine cents and ladies' dress shoes with heels and bows were a dollar ninety-eight. Goldstein and Cohen was the most popular store in Ensley. (It is still there and doing well.) Penney's ran a close second. Cotton's, another old-timer, is still in business. Kress and Silvers (the five and dime stores) faded from Ensley many years ago.

Occasionally we had need for a loaf of store-bought bread. A loaf, unsliced, was 10 cents.

For refrigeration we had an ice box. An ice man came around daily. A dime's worth would last all day if the weather was not too hot and if we used it sparingly. An ice pick was used to chip off pieces as needed. Children gathered around the truck at every stop begging for ice chips that fell from the blocks as they were cut to be delivered.

What happened to sunflowers! They used to dot the vacant lots and stand elegantly beside the alleyways of my youth.

I wish that I could return to that cherished part of my life when Fairfield and Ensley — unknowingly — held for me the wealth of the world.

RALPH HAMMOND

❧ ❧ ❧

Valley Head, Alabama

V alley Head is unique in many ways. It is nestled at the foot of Lookout Mountain, and in the days when Mentone was a great tourist attraction, Valley Head was the train stop where all the folk from New Orleans and Birmingham got off for a four-mile ride up the mountainside to the healthful springs that flowed at the brow of the mountain, there beside the Mentone Springs Hotel. My father operated a livery stable, and with horse-drawn surries transported the vacationing guests up and down the mountain.

One day as I was riding with him, he killed a huge rattlesnake in the roadway just as he was curving his surrey into the unloading zone of the hotel. He picked it up and took it toward the hotel's back entrance, where he coiled it up and placed a coat over it. Then he yelled for the Negro porter to come out from the hotel, and when the porter bounced out of the door, papa told him to pick up that coat. That black man almost jumped over the hotel when he saw the snake!

Valley Head was a thriving town long before the Alabama Great Southern Railroad was ever built. In fact, William Overton Winston of Valley Head was one of the prime movers who got the railroad built. When it had been completed from Chattanooga to Allen's Switch, halfway between Valley Head and Fort Payne, the promoters of the railroad sponsored a 4th of July picnic at the big spring at Allen. The train came loaded down with financial backers from Chattanooga, but after the party there was no place for the train to turn around, so it had to back all the way to Chattanooga. One person attending that party was my kinsman, Cassius Caius Davenport, who died in the late '30s. Cassie had been a bugle boy in the Civil War, and he once told me about how those attending the Allen party got drunk on a barrel of "cherry bounce," and many got into a Wild West fight which soon broke up the festivities.

But more than almost anything else about Valley Head, I remember the cold winters. Our big house had a double fireplace, back to back, and we'd keep the logs roaring in the dead of winter. I remember that we'd stand in front of the fire and almost toast ourselves, while the other side would almost freeze. That was long before there were any daily weather reports, which in recent years have reported Valley Head to be the coldest place in the state.

The sounds of Valley Head always intrigued me. Folks for a couple of miles around geared their lives to the whistle-blowing of Uncle Doc White's sawmill whistle. It was very shrill, and its blast cut through the ridges and up and down the valleys, telling people that it was time to go to work, or time to quit.

The smells of the place made for equally lasting memories: the smell of Jim Reynolds' homemade chili as you cracked the door open and entered his cafe. One day when ordering a bowl of his renowned chili, I noticed as he brought it toward me that he had his thumb stuck in it. I said to him: "Mr. Reynolds, you've got your thumb stuck in my chili!" He replied, "That's all right, it ain't hot."

But the most lingering smell was always emanating from Terry Hoot Wright's barber shop. Mr. Wright had gone off to Terre Haute, Indiana, and got a job barbering for a while, and when he returned home, he became known as "Terry Hoot." Well, he had some kind of catarrh, and he smoked a stinking tobacco that could be smelled a block away. I always cramped my thumb and index finger over my nose while passing his shop.

And then there were the tastes that will always be reminders of growing up in Valley Head. The raisin pies, piled high with browned meringue, that Carl Sloan made in his restaurant, year after year. And the vanilla milkshakes that Jim Hall spun out at the Valley Head Drug Store, left with just the right size lumps of vanilla ice cream floating around in them. And the aroma floating out of Rachael Reece's kitchen when she was baking her famous angel food cakes — times when she'd run all of us playful kids out into the yard at baking time, for fear that we'd shake the house as we played, and make her lighter-than-feather cakes fall.

And what grandson could ever forget the kitchen smells of a grandmother like my Grandma Susannah Warren Holleman who lived a few miles away on Sand Mountain. Somehow Grandma had a special liking for me — always calling me R.C. — and I'd spend many visits with her and Grandpa before I was old enough to start to school. On one of those visits, Grandma, knowing how much I liked Irish potatoes, told me, "R.C., you're going to spend a week with us, and you know what? I'm going to cook Irish potatoes for you every meal — three meals a day, for seven days — and every meal they're going to be cooked different — all 21 times!" And she did, and did I enjoy every bite of them.

I especially remember the times at Christmas when there was always a barrel of Yates apples stored in the barn loft among the hay, and Grandma could munch on those apples better than a squirrel. It thrilled me just to watch her eat one of those Yates apples — thrilled me so much, that years later I wrote a short story about her, called "My Red-Apple Granny" which was published in *Southern Farmer* magazine. On one of my visits with Grandma, I got sulled up and pouted for some reason long forgotten, but I remember that I hid under the big dining room table. Granny, sensing my condition, got her a pan of apples to peel, and sat at the table, where she soon began to sing a little song that went like this: "Joe, Joe, cut off his toe, and hung it up to dry; the boys and girls came along and laughed and old Joe cried!" She had hardly finished singing it, when I peered out from under the tablecloth and said, "Sing that again, Granny!" And she did. That song became a party of my lifetime singing repertoire.

And oh the teacake smells of Aunt Kate Winston's baking! She was related to my Grandma, both of them coming from Girltown, Alabama, midway between Fort Payne and Valley Head in Big Willis Valley, at the location where the Terrapin Hills Golf Course is now situated. Aunt Kate was married to Dr. John Winston, and they had a beautiful Italianate mansion built back into the ridgeside, just as you enter Valley Head from the gap in the ridge. Aunt Kate would often be waiting on the verandah, with a cookie jar filled with her freshly made cookies, and when I'd saunter along toward home from school, she'd often call out to me, "You're Alice's boy, aren't you? Well, come on up and have some cookies!" Quite a few years ago her house was bought and dismantled and moved to Birmingham where it became the home of Mr. and Mrs. Edwin Cole at 3377 Cherokee Road.

(It has nothing to do with smells, but a bit of my early history was made there on the tall row of steps leading up to Aunt Kate's house. It was Thanksgiving Day and the big annual turkey trot was in progress, when they threw out a guinea from atop the bank building. That old guinea sailed and sailed, finally coming down in a clump of honeysuckle vines there atop Aunt Kate's steps. Paul Burnett and I were both rushing in to capture that guinea, and some way, I got my hands on her legs and pulled her out first, claiming her for my very own. At that point, Paul looked over the watching crowd and yelled, "Ralph Charlie Cotch A Guinea In The Bush!" And that became my nickname for years thereafter — if you can believe it.)

And oh the taste of Annie Ruth Davenport's potato salad which she always brought to the annual Methodist picnic at Fred and Imogene Huron's Riverside Hotel! Somehow Miss Annie Ruth could mix the right amount of potatoes and onions and mayonnaise, and whatever other stuff she used — in just the right proportions. And hers was the first dish I always headed for after the preacher had graced the dinner-on-the-ground.

And my own dear mother's great apple turnover pies. Some way she'd always make three oversize turnovers, I suppose because she had a big platter that the three just fit into, and then she'd dribble some sort of creamed sugary frosting across the top. Never before or since have I ever seen anyone make such turnovers. And how the company always raved over that dessert. It was almost as popular as her apple stack cake, the several cake layers being flavored sharply with sorghum molasses, and sugared dried apples used for filling between the layers.

And how could I ever forget that crockful of brandied peaches? That's what old Uncle Ned Jackson, who, while living on the overlook rim of Lookout Mountain at the site where Cragsmere restaurant is now located, served to my papa and me early one Christmas day when papa stopped to see if Uncle Ned had seen anything of a foxhound that had failed to return from the race the night before. Uncle Ned escorted us to a little covered shed where he carefully spooned out a cupful of peaches, ladling the brandied juice to the rim of the cup, and handed it to papa. Then with his long beard gleaming white against his black skin, he looked at papa sheepishly and asked, "You don't mind if the little boy celebrates Christmas with just one brandied peach, do you Mr. Bleve?" And what could papa say to such a pleading, but yes? So I got my first taste of any kind of alcohol on that eventful Christmas morning.

Besides the Winston Italianate mansion, there were other such mansions in Valley Head, one being Hampshire House, a big rambling two-story affair with more gables than Hawthorne's seven. For a time Ida Beulah Dean operated it as a boarding house, mostly for drummers who'd come into Valley Head with samples of merchandise to sell to Uncle Nick Davenport's big mercantile store — the largest such store in the northern half of the county. And as I'd walk to and from school, I walked along the trail that bordered the fence around Hampshire House on two sides, and Ida Beulah's old dog Bruno — a wild and woolly canine — took great pleasure in barking and yapping and chasing me all the way around the fence. One day when he chased me to the far end of the yard, next to the barn, I figured I'd get even with Old Bruno, so while he barked at me fiercely, showing his snarling teeth, I made water upon him through the latticed fence!

But the biggest mansion in town was Winston Place, the original rooms of which were built by Dr. Gardner, but later added to with imposing quality by William Overton Winston, using largely slave labor for the task . . . Mr. Winston himself being related to Winston Churchill's mother from Virginia! In later generations, through marriages, the mansion was lived in by the Andersons and Tutwilers from Birmingham. It was by far the most imposing mansion in the county. At the end of World War II my oldest brother, Haralson Hammond, bought the home from the Tutwilers, and it is today the residence of his daughter, La Jean Hammond, the wife of retired Colonel Welborn Matthews. The mansion has a massive verandah with four huge Doric columns, and is set in a grove of cedar and oak and beechnut trees.

I well remember one day back in the late '20s when Jacqueline Tutwiler drove her red Cadillac touring car down to Valley Head's one dog-leg street, and parked it beside the railroad depot's flower garden. But when she got out and started to walk down the sidewalk and into the drugstore, the policeman noticed that she didn't have on any stockings! When he threatened to arrest her for "indecent exposure" she gave him a bawling out which didn't sound too much like a lady! Indeed it was the language that wasn't often heard on the streets of Valley Head, especially from a woman.

On another occasion, Jacqueline, when trying to turn around in the road, backed her Cadillac off the edge of the mountain, greatly damaging it. Elmer Dalby, the master mechanic of the town, towed it to his garage. After a long fixing-up he brought it over to the new U.S. 11 highway that had just been built through what is now Hammondville, where he told the men to halt all passing traffic at the place, for he was going to see how fast Jackie's Cadillac would run. Well, Elmer drove west and turned around in Lowry's big yard, and when he topped Lowry's Hill heading our way, a great cloud of dust was boiling up behind him on the dirt road. And when he came roaring through the crossroads, we all cheered him wildly, for we'd never before seen a car go that fast. When he shortly returned, he said, "Boys, I saw it on 95!"

And what excitement there was in town back in the summer of 1919 when wings fell on Valley Head. In fact, the town hadn't seen so many people since the Yankees went through en route to battles around Chattanooga during the Civil War. There was a forced airplane landing by Kathryn Stinson, one of America's pioneer women pilots, whose family made the Stinson airplanes. With her motor sputtering she sailed down into the Winston pasture, clipping off tree tops as she descended. My brother Haralson and L.P. Dean (later an NBC radio announcer in New York) were the first to reach the plane, which had landed nose-down and tail-up, and they helped the pilot down from her perch in the air. I was only four years old at the time, and when Miss Stinson hired my papa to patrol the plane and keep it safe from the horde of sightseers while she sent for parts from Chattanooga, I had one of the great experiences of my life. My papa held me up and let me sit in the cockpit of that flying ginny. No jet-age pilot of later times ever felt more important with up-in-the-cloud happiness than I did that eventful day in Valley Head.

I had just started in the primer (as we used to call the first year in school) at the big two-store white schoolhouse on the day that my brother Alva got a new nickname. As usual sister Emma carried a syrup bucket filled with our lunch, and after she'd passed it out to my three brothers and me, we all dashed off into one of the big red clay ditches at least 20 feet deep, where we all sat around and ate lunch. Somehow on that day, Haralson, my oldest brother, got into an argument with Johnny Tate (who for many years operated a barber shop in Homewood), and when the two began to have very strong words, brother Alva picked up a big baked sweet potato from his lunch, and yelled at Johnny, "If you don't let my brother alone, I'm gonna throw this BUZZING 'TATER at you!" And that broke up the argument, as everybody began laughing at Alva's BUZZING 'TATER! And for years later he was called "Buzzing 'Tater" by the boys at school.

Up in the loft of Cousin Belle Hamman's old livery stable (which papa had operated earlier on), there was a pair of old coffins that had been there for years, and it seemed that almost everyone knew about those coffins, for they some way cast a gloom into conversation when folks even dared to talk about them. On several occasions, while trekking home from school, I'd detour a bit and climb the stairs into that barnlike loft. I'd mosey up to those coffins and stare at them, my body trembling with fear. And then — one day when bravery overcame the reticence of valor — I did it. I eased open the lid of one coffin, and ever so slowly lowered my body into it — not daring to close the lid, for I knew if it snapped shut there was no way to open it from the inside. I just wanted to feel what it was like to be dead. What a ghostly feeling that was. And you can bet I never tried that again.

All these things remembered, and many, many more not told, made a lasting impression upon my youthful mind. I saw a little valley — set down in a very special way. It was my very own town, for I was born there in the white cottage that still stands beside Winston Memorial Presbyterian Church. And the recollection of things remembered has stoked my mind over the long years, feeding it with a never-ending source of life and human nature.

Somehow, there is a mystique about the town. It is slow-paced and deep-seated and accepts change very sparingly. And too there is a quiet elegance about the place and its people — both black and white — who long before the Civil War learned to live together as family.

FRANK THEODORE KANELOS

🐦 🐦 🐦

Birmingham, Alabama

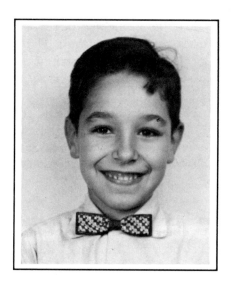

I t is indeed a pleasure recalling memories of growing up in Alabama.

I was a post-World War II baby born in Birmingham in 1948 at West End Baptist Hospital, now Baptist Medical Center-Princeton. My mother was a native of Fairfield. My father was born in Newport News, Virginia, where he lived until the War brought him to Fort McClelland in Anniston. My parents met at my aunt and uncle's "Anniston Restaurant" and were later married in Birmingham at the Holy Trinity Greek Orthodox Church in 1944. The church has since been torn down and a new cathedral built. After an army tour of duty in Europe, my father returned to Birmingham where my parents made their home. My father died in 1971. My mother still lives here.

Growing up in Idlewild Hills was an adventure of sorts in the '50s. Red Mountain was pretty much virgin territory. Valley Avenue was not built up, and the condominiums that now stand at the crest of the mountain were not there. Our house faced the downtown Birmingham side of the mountain. On clear nights in the fall and winter we could look out our windows and see the skyline of the city lighted up like a Christmas tree. Some of my early beginnings as a poet were inspired by this view. It was at this time that I began to love Birmingham.

On the other side of our home was the side of Red Mountain. It was essentially a forest, my very own forest. The neighbor children and I would explore every nook and cranny, every secret hollow and rock. We played in an abandoned "cave" which I believe in reality was an abandoned mining area. There were remnants of railroad tracks where we used to play. If we hiked to the crest of the mountain we would be standing where the condominiums now stand off Valley Avenue near Beacon Parkway. To us it was the "Wild West." We always expected to see Indians at any moment or to at least find some arrowheads. We never did.

It was a very conservative time for Birmingham. It was probably suburbia in its infancy. Every house had young children running down the street or riding bicycles, no ten-speeds. We could be seen playing baseball, cowboys and Indians, kickball, or roller skating down the hills.

I attended Glen Iris Elementary School. It was a place full of tradition. So many of my cousins went there. The teachers were dedicated and often retired there after many years of service to the school system. In a recent conversation with the receptionist at my office, I realized we had the same eighth grade teacher at Glen Iris. My receptionist and I are about twenty years apart in age.

It was during my grade school days that I discovered the movies. I was either at the Mickey Mouse Club at the Alabama Theater or at the Ritz, the Empire, the Strand, the Melba, or the Lyric. I began a love affair with Hollywood which I still have. I could get in for thirty-five cents then. I always had a dime to buy a Mars bar or fifteen cents for popcorn. The Alabama, the Lyric, and the Melba are the only buildings left standing. I really miss my old friends.

My family used to take rides and get ice cream in the evenings. I best remember the Polar Bear Spinning Wheel on First Avenue in East Lake and the Spinning Wheel on Twentieth Street South. Sometimes we would go to the Tutwiler Hotel pharmacy and get a milkshake. My father and I proclaimed those the very best in Birmingham.

Television emerged on the scene, fascinating and mysterious. My favorites were "Howdy Doody," "Ding Dong School," "Captain Kangaroo" (God bless him), "Twinkie," and "Mighty Mouse." I recall the first television show I saw in color. It was "Peter Pan" with Mary Martin. This had the same impact that watching our first walk on the moon had on me; disbelief, joy, and amazement.

Another strong memory was of Sunday dinners with the family. It was almost taken for granted that we would all congregate at one of my aunt's houses and feast on numerous goodies. We always took a large plate of food home with us. At the dinner table we would recall events from the past. My aunts and uncles would sit around relating stories of early Fairfield and of Greece.

My paternal grandparents were from Sparta, an area not too far from Athens, Greece. They emigrated to Newport News, Virginia, and remained there until their deaths. My maternal grandparents were from an island in Greece called Chios. My grandfather came to Fairfield (Fairfield was then called Cory) in 1903. He worked as a rigger at U.S. Steel for several years. My grandmother and her first child came to Fairfield about three years later. In the following years my grandparents had six more children all delivered at home with the assistance of Dr. Carmichael's granddaughter (a physical therapist) at United Cerebral Palsy in Birmingham.

Grandfather later opened his own business in Fairfield. It was a small cafe at the end of the streetcar line at U.S. Steel. Several of mother's uncles also had businesses in Fairfield. These included a bakery, a fruit stand, and a confectionery.

My mother remembers during the Depression having to join several of her siblings to help their father sell gum, candy, tobacco, and doughnuts to the U.S. Steel workers as they would go to work in the mornings. The children would wake up about five a.m., work, then go to school. It was a difficult time for the family. Money and food were always provided though sometimes difficult to obtain. My grandparents saw to it that the children always had good food, even if it meant cutting back in some other way. My grandfather would sometimes wait until everyone had finished eating before he ate from the leftovers on each plate. I can't help but marvel at the amount of love that existed there in that home. Laughter was plentiful as well as strong cooperation, sharing, and religious conviction. Sometimes neighbors would share their excess or trade items to even out the distribution of scarce goods. The children shared in the chores of washing clothes on the open fire, of scrubbing clothes on the scrub board, of tending to the garden, of raising and slaughtering the animals (chickens, ducks, goats, sheep, rabbits, pigeons), and of cooking and baking bread.

The family lived at two locations in Fairfield, on 51st Street, then on 56th Street. In 1944 tragedy struck the family three times. My grandfather died of a heart attack and two of his sons died in action in Europe during World War II. After the War my grandmother moved to Southside where she eventually died in 1953.

I will end my remembrance with a childhood memory of my mother as she related it to me.

"We used to play hopscotch, baseball, kickball, and hide-and-go-seek. We would often go hiking in the woods to hunt wild hickory nuts, blackberries, sassafras, persimmons, and pecans. It was always a treat to ride the trolley to East Lake Park and spend the day. We saved our Orange Crush bottle tops so we could ride the rides, then we would have a picnic. But what I remember most is the May Day Festival. It was always a special time of year. I will never forget the Maypole. It all still lingers in my heart."

IRMA R. CRUSE

ð ð ð

Hackneyville, Alabama

The early morning sun was shining so brightly across the lattice-work around the back porch that I had to squint to see my two tall, lanky blonde uncles. They had hitched their mules to the big hook at the end of the porch, close to the well, and I heard Uncle Harlan call: "Nellie, tell Irma to come out here; we have something for her."

I jumped up from the breakfast table when I heard them ride up, laughing and talking to each other. Harlan was twenty and Andrew was seventeen, but they were grown-up men so far as I was concerned. I liked it when they took time to talk to me. I stood still at the kitchen door, waiting expectantly, as they took the back steps two at a time. Uncle Andrew got to me first and he said: "Close your eyes and hold out your hand."

I closed my eyes obediently. It wasn't easy, for Mamma had plaited my two brown pigtails so tight that it pulled the skin across my forehead when I closed my eyes. I always did what my uncles told me to, just as I did whatever Mamma and Papa said. I knew that little girls were supposed to mind grown-ups.

"All right, you can open your eyes now. Happy birthday, little four-year-old!" Andrew said that, but Harlan corrected him:

"You mean great big four-year-old, don't you?"

I opened my eyes and looked.

There were four shiny pennies in my hand.

"Four pennies for your birthday. One for each year. Hold them tight and don't drop them."

I closed my fingers over the pennies and lifted my face for the kiss the uncles always gave me when they came. One of the pennies fell, bounced once, and rolled through a crack in the back porch floor to the ground underneath.

I didn't mean to cry, but they had told me to hold the money and I had dropped it. I didn't know what to say, and I looked down, trying to hide the tear that came rolling down my face and onto my brown-checked dress. Babies cried and I was big — four years old — but I had done wrong and I knew it.

"Hey, don't cry. I'll go find the money. Just hold on to the others and don't drop them. They are yours to spend because you have a birthday."

Uncle Andrew dashed down the back steps and crawled under the flooring. It was easy for him to get through the opening in the lattice-work underpinning. He came out almost at once, holding the penny up for me to see. Mamma, Papa, and Ellaree had followed me out of the kitchen and were watching. Ellaree was standing behind Mamma, looking out from behind her skirt. They were all looking at me and smiling now.

Strange how the memory of that incident remained vivid through the years! I cannot remember what I bought with my money. Nor can I remember a birthday cake or a celebration of any kind. There was just that awful sinking feeling because I had dropped the money. I was a bad, clumsy girl.

There were other memories of those early years but they are not sharp and clear like the incident of the birthday pennies. The memories are nearly always associated with the weather. I think of the things that happened and associate them with sunny days, or cold days, or rainy, damp days.

I remember the early spring morning when Papa hitched up the old mule and plowed the ground for the kitchen garden. I found a sunny spot against the fence among the pink and purple hyacinths where the wind did not blow. I was shivering as I pulled my blue sweater tight across my chest, but I did not want to go inside. I could hear a robin singing in an apple tree; I could hear the click of metal against rock as the plow moved through the winter-roughened ground.

"Come in, Irma, and get warm," Mamma called. "Ellaree is eating her breakfast. Come get yours while it's hot." I didn't want to go inside. I liked standing there where I could watch my father and smell the freshness of that garden soil. I liked to look at the long worms that the plow turned up. I wanted to reach out and touch one of the wiggly worms. But Mamma had said to come in. I bent over to get a long whiff of the sweetness of the pink hyacinth and turned toward the house.

There was another memory. It was late morning and the sun was shining. I was out in the orchard where the apple trees and peach trees grew. Up toward the top of the hill was a scuppernong arbor, and circling the arbor were three or four pear trees, white with early blossoms. I was holding Ellaree by the hand, pulling her along the furrows between the rows of fruit trees. We were hunting for her bottle, her milk bottle, and we couldn't find it. Ellaree was crying, her blonde curls tousled in the light breeze, and her blue eyes reddened by tears. Now and then her little baby-body would shake with a gulping, deep-down sob. Mamma had told me to look after her; now we had lost her bottle. I knew I couldn't go back to the house without it.

As I look back and try to remember, I do not know whether we found the bottle. All I remember is that agonizing search.

Guests came to the Charlie Russell house often. The big rambling two-story house had plenty of bedrooms for people to spend the night. I liked knowing that my father was the oldest child in his family, for I was the oldest grandchild and that seemed to make me important. All the Russell kin came to see us and spent a lot of time talking to me or playing with me, and with Ellaree after she was big enough to get off Mamma's lap and play, too.

Mamma Belle, my grandmother Russell, would come in the big buggy with Aunt Allie, my father's fourteen-year-old sister, riding with her. Uncle Harlan and Uncle Andrew usually rode the mules and would stop by for a meal or just to play with my sister and me. Aunt Allie did not seem like a real aunt for she would sit on the floor and play dolls with us. Uncle Tommy and Aunt Julia were more like "real" aunt and uncle for they were grown and married and lived in their own house at Alexander City. They had a little boy, my cousin, S.T., a year younger than I was.

We had other kinfolks, too. There were great-aunts, second and third cousins, and some I was never sure about, except that I knew they were kin to us. Mamma Belle was the only grandmother. Most of my playmates had two grandmothers. I asked Mamma about that. She said my other grandmother, her own mother, was dead. I learned that both my grandfathers were dead. I didn't understand what that meant but I began to understand as I got older.

Sometimes company came at mealtime. After dinner or supper, they would all go out on the front porch if the weather was warm. When it was cold, they would sit around the fireplace in the big front room. There was a lot of hugging and kissing when the kinfolks came. They would look at Ellaree and me, talk about who we favored, stand us off so they could see us better, and then tell us to go play while they talked.

I would mind them and go play but I would come in and out of the room where they were talking and I could hear snatches of their conversation. I remember the time one of the grown-up cousins (twice removed) got out of the buggy in the backyard and called out to Mamma:

"Nellie, I've got to see your girls. Tell them to come kiss their Cousin Hattie."

I walked toward the strange lady obediently. She gave me a big hug and then held me away from her. "Well, that's Charlie Russell, as I live and breathe!" That was a strange thing for her to say.

When Mamma went to the kitchen to fix supper, I went to the

kitchen, too. "Mamma, that lady thought I was Papa. Didn't she know my name?"

There were so many kinfolks coming and going that the "company at mealtime" routine was accepted by all of us. It was interesting to watch Mamma go out in the backyard, catch two fryers, swing them round and round in an operation that she called "wringing their necks." She would let me stand to one side while the chickens flopped helplessly around the yard until they died. As I got older, I still did not understand how the chicken could keep moving so long after its neck was broken. Others who helped prepare meals would use the axe to cut off the heads of the fowls, but Mamma always explained apologetically:

"I just can't bear to cut off the head of a chicken."

I did not understand why she considered it more merciful to wring the fryer's neck.

There were two members of our household during those early years that I can barely remember, but whose names were mentioned often. They were "Uncle Turner" and "Aunt Jane." One day when I was talking to Aunt Julia, I asked her:

"Are Uncle Turner and Aunt Jane my aunt and uncle like you and Uncle Tommy are?"

"No, child, we just call them by those names as a term of affection. Uncle Turner is your father's grandfather, and Aunt Jane is your father's step-grandmother."

That was entirely too complicated for me to understand. I knew that Mamma Belle was my grandmother and that she was also my father's mother. But how could Papa have a grandfather? And what was a step-grandmother? Mamma Belle's name was Russell just like my name. Why, then, did her father have the name of "Turner Ray" instead of Russell?

Uncle Turner was kind and loving and he had a long beard. He talked to me about "the War." On sunny days he would walk with his cane down the road to Papa's store. A few times he let me walk with him. We sat on a bench in front of the store with other men who had long beards and who walked with canes. They told stories about fighting. After I went to school and studied history, I understood that they had been talking about the War Between the States and the Spanish-American War.

I was only four when Uncle Turner died. I know now that the family tried to protect Ellaree and me from the pain of death of our loved ones. At the time, I did not know what had happened but Uncle Turner just wasn't there any more. The only definite memory of Aunt Jane came through a series of incidents when Aunt Allie had come to live with us. I remember that she would come running into the house, calling Mamma.

"Nellie, come quick. Aunt Jane is down and can't get up."

Mamma would run to the backyard where Aunt Jane would be on her knees at the woodpile. The old woman in her eighties would have an armload of stovewood, and would be unable to get up without help. I heard one of the neighbors talking and she said: "Jane is too stubborn to put the wood down and get up by herself."

Aunt Jane must have died within the next year, for there are no further memories of her. Another thing I wondered about as I got older was why these great-grandparents came to live with us, instead of with Mamma Belle or with one of Uncle Turner's other children.

There are all sorts of isolated incidents stored away in my memory of my childhood. In one of them, I was playing contentedly with a carefully tied onion set when Mamma asked me where I got the little bundle of fresh green and white plants.

"I just found them, Mamma. They were on Mrs. Ware's front porch. I was playing with Mildred and Herman and when I started home, I saw them. I tiptoed up on the porch so I wouldn't bother anybody and got me a bunch of them so I could plant me a garden."

"Mrs. Ware did not give you those onions. You will have to take them back right now. Don't ever take something that does not belong to you. That is stealing. Take them back and I'll wait here on the front porch for you."

I could tell that Mamma was upset. It made me feel real bad for her to be upset with me, and I couldn't help sobbing as I walked across the front yard, and slid down the red clay bank to the road. I wiped my eyes with the hem of my dress, and walked up the path to the clean-swept yard of the Ware home. I remember climbing over the brush broom that was laying across the steps to the porch. I knocked on the door, scared, and not sure what I was supposed to say.

When Mrs. Ware opened the screen and looked out, I handed her the onion sets.

"Mamma said I had to bring these back to you. I didn't mean to steal them."

Mrs. Ware just stood there looking at me. Then she said: "That's all right this time, child. Thank you."

I ran fast across the road and up the bank under the cedar trees to the front porch of our house.

I played at the Wares nearly every day. Most of the time, when Mildred Ware and I played, her brothers, Herman and Lanier, would not play with us. The eight-and ten-year-old boys did not like to make playhouses and play dolls. That is what Mildred and I liked to do most of all. But one day while we were playing, putting our dolls to bed, and making mud pies for supper, Herman and Lanier started a new game.

They would slip up behind us, pull up our skirts, laugh real loud, then run and hide behind the barn. In a few minutes, they would come back and go through that same procedure. I remember that I was trying to get the playhouse in order, with all the dishes lined up in a straight row, and the pinestraw chairs properly turned at just the right angle. It was aggravating when the boys ran by, flipped up my dress, and said, "O-wee" and ran off again, laughing hard.

I did not see why that was so funny, but I had an uneasy feeling that Mrs. Ware wouldn't like it if she saw them. I felt sure that Mamma would make me come home if she looked across the road and saw what was going on. When I went home that afternoon, I thought about the boys and their game. I thought I'd ask Mamma why they acted that way, but I had a strange feeling that it wasn't the kind of thing I should mention to her.

I began to learn more about what was expected of me when kinfolks came. I tried to understand some of the strange things people said to me. I remember the time another elderly cousin came to visit from out of town. She had not been there since Ellaree was born, and I did not remember her at all.

"Irma and Ellaree, come see Cousin Carrie. She wants to meet you." Mamma waited for us to come in, smiling proudly as her little girls entered.

I was the first in the room.

"So this is Irma! Well, my dear, how do you do?" She reached out to shake hands. It always made me a little uncomfortable to shake hands with grown people, but they seemed to like to do it; that is, when they were not hugging and kissing.

Cousin Carrie turned to Ellaree.

"And this is the pretty one! Come see Cousin Carrie, Ellaree. Let me look at those curls."

Soon after that, I heard Mamma talking to Aunt Julia about me.

"Irma has started walking in her sleep. I don't understand it. She has always been such a sound sleeper. Do you know that the other night, I heard a sound and got out of bed. That child was standing up on the hall tree, looking in the mirror, and crying in her sleep."

I heard Aunt Julia telling another story and I remember it.

"When Ellaree was born and Nellie had typhoid fever, I took Irma down to my house for a visit. She was just seventeen months old when the new baby came, but she could talk. She would follow me around as I did my housework, asking questions, and telling me about her mother and father, and about the uncles and about Allie, Charlie's little sister."

Aunt Julia would laugh as she finished her story:

"Irma could talk real plain, and it was interesting to say a new word and hear her repeat it. One afternoon I was transplanting nasturtiums. 'What are those, Aunt Julia?' she asked me. I had no idea she could say a long word like that, but I answere her question seriously. 'Those are nasturtiums, Irma,' I told her. That child walked around the rest of the afternoon saying 'nasturtiums' to herself."

It made me feel good to hear that story. I remember Aunt Julia told it soon after I began walking in my sleep. It sounded like she thought it was good that I could say big words when I was a year-and-a-half old.

When I was five years old, two school teachers came to board in the big house with us. They lived out about six or seven miles from Hackneyville, too far to drive in the buggy to school every day. I liked having teachers live with us. It was like having the preacher live in your house. I could tell my playmates thought it was special to have teachers live in your home.

When Miss Lavelle and her sister came in from school in the afternoon, they would play with Ellaree and me a while before they went to their rooms to get ready for the next day.

After a few weeks, Miss Lavelle talked to Mamma and I heard her. I was putting my dolls to bed and the door was open to Mamma's room. The teacher was saying:

"Mrs. Russell, I believe Irma would do all right in school if you'd let me take her with me for a few days. She is trying so hard to read that it would be a shame not to give her this chance. I can put her in the primer class and see how she gets along."

I almost held my breath for fear Mamma would say no.

She said she would talk to Papa and let Miss Lavelle know. The next day, Mamma told me that if I would be good and mind Miss Lavelle, I could go to school with her and see how I liked it.

School! They had books at school. We didn't have books at our house — at least, none that I knew about. We had catalogs and sometimes a copy of a newspaper called *The Alexander City Outlook*.

So I started to school at five and a half. I was allowed to look on with the other children in the primer class and try to read their books.

One day in early spring, just before school was out, the teacher brought a package to class. She let the pupils open the package. Inside were picture books.

"I ordered these from Birmingham," she told us. "They cost ten cents apiece and there is one for each of you. You must be careful and wash your hands before you read them. Don't tear them for I can't get any more for you this year."

After all the other pupils got their books, Miss Lavelle handed one to me. My book was "The Little Red Hen."

That was the first book I ever owned. I read it over and over until I knew it by heart.

As I looked at those pictures and read the book to Ellaree, I wished for more books like that one. One day I told Mamma:

"Please ask Papa to buy me another book. When I get grown, I'm going to have books all over my house — in every single room."

MARK CHILDRESS

ềề ề ề

Monroeville, Alabama

I n Alabama, women fish.

This is not to say that women elsewhere do not fish, that Alabama fisherwomen catch larger fish, or that fishing is somehow an inappropriate pastime for women. But the women of Alabama fish with a peculiar settled attitude that removes fishing from the realm of sport and makes it a kind of reflective necessity, like putting up figs or going to church.

I stand on the crumbling red clay bank of Bates' Pond, near Fort Deposit in that time-battered, kudzu-choked land known as the Black Belt. Seated before me, on a canvas camp stool, shaded by her wide straw hat, a cane pole planted in the mud beside a cardboard cup roiling with Red Wigglers, is Cora Estelle Freeman Gillion, my grandmother, whose greatest joy was to fish.

Her squat white Rambler station wagon is parked a few feet away, tailgate unfolded, supporting all she needs for a day at the pond. There is an ingenious wire cricket-cage with its open mouth that mysteriously prohibits escape, since crickets cannot leap straight up. Its small cheeping prisoners ricochet with tiny pings against its sides. Lunch is a crumpling of tinfoil, holding a handful of flour biscuit, and a blue plastic jug filled with tepid spigot-water.

Most intriguing of all, to my chubby hands, is her tackle box. The box itself is unexceptional with its clasp shut. But once open, it is a jewel-box, bursting with dangerous fingerpricking fishhooks, dreamily colored lures (never removed from their cellophane, since she favors worms, crickets, and occasionally a used wad of Juicy Fruit), all manner of glistening weights and strings, corks, a sprinkling of iridescent fish-scales, the cleaning-knife with its raw ugly serration, bobbers, plungers, hand scales and, safely stowed in one of the tiny compartments that glide up when the box is opened, her old worn wedding ring.

Strapped to the Rambler's flank is a thatch of fishing poles like primitive antennae — bamboo canes in several lengths, and a selection of expensive rods given as presents by her children, tied to the car and promptly forgotten. Circling the wagon, leaving his moist mark on all four tires, is Adolf the german shepherd (wittily named by my aunt, but as sweet a pacifist as you could find). Adolf is company, friend, and conversation, and consistently fetches back the undersized fish Grandmother tosses into the weeds nearby.

The result of damming a muddy creek, Bates' Pond is a muddy oval surrounded by tall pines in varied burnt-out shades of green. On Fourths of July, Bateses and Freemans and Gillions line the bank, lazily trailing their lines on the water, while those of us too young to be embarrassed by our underwear splash and churn in the fertile water. But this is another day, and as on any other day, Stella Gillion has come to fish in peace.

It does not matter what she will catch, or even if she catches nothing. In my mind, great pikes and whales cruise just below the dun-colored surface, waiting for the single worm that will make them lunge, but Grandmother knows ponds and holds no such illusions. Her joy is in this sitting and watching, listening to the tweedle of the insect symphony, alone by a pond that will yield only an occasional catfish or blue-gill.

The best thing that can happen does: the red-and-white bobber shakes its nervous head, quivers, holds still again a moment, then is sucked down through still water and disappears.

"Oh sweet," she calls to Adolf, "would you looka there!" She unfolds from the washtub, pulling the pole from the mud with a small sucking sound, twisting her wrist, answering the pull from below with one of her own. "Lawd I bet he's three pounds! Come on, now, baby, here come some dinner!"

With a mild tug, and a croon for the fish, she lofts her pole, and up it comes, a catfish already gone limp in surrender, curling its tail just a little as it swings into her hand. Grandmother dons one glove, to fend off his razory spines and wraps her satisfied hand around the slimy, substantial body.

"And cain't you near bout taste him," she says to herself, then turns to me for congratulation. I applaud, for I am afraid of all fish and she has conquered this one. I jump to pull up the other string anchored in the bank, with its wriggling catch of sunfish and red-ears twice-hooked, and Grandmother adds the cat. They are lowered again into the pond's edge, awaiting the end of the day and the slow flapping death in the Rambler's floorboard, and the dusting of corn meal, and the hot oil.

The phone may be ringing when Grandmother returns to her house, and if it is, it is my mother or another of her children, worried half to death because she called and called all day and got no answer. And Grandmother will laugh in that loud hee-haw, and say she was just fishing.

Fishing is the only escape from the ring of the phone, and the unsettling news, good or bad, that always follows. And from electric power, and indoor plumbing (over the fence, in the weeds, does just fine), and from shade, and comfort, and from any other living person except the ones she chooses to take along.

Once or twice the person she chose was me, and when we talked, it was of odd things — horses she rode as a child, the assassinations which were at that time still surprising, the day my mother was born, how to kill a chicken without making it squawk.

But never of fish or fishing. They were beyond conversation, and any discussion would have dampened her joy.

The shellcrackers she caught existed in Bates' Pond so she could catch them, and cook them, and feed herself and her children, so they could grow and have their own children, who might prefer the dazzle of a Florida beach to the somnolence of Bates' Pond. When there were no more children to feed, Grandmother snagged with her cane pole and her worms the times when there were.

NOTES ON CONTRIBUTORS

Dr. Richard Arrington, Jr., a former teacher, biologist, and Executive Director of the Alabama Center for Higher Education, served on the Birmingham City Council from 1971-1979. In October, 1979, he was elected Mayor of Birmingham — the first black to hold the office.

Gould Beech was editor of the *Montgomery Advertiser* from 1934-1936 and 1940-1942, and editor of the *Southern Farmer* from 1946-1948. Now semi-retired, he lives in Magnolia Springs, Alabama, where he is active in real estate.

Nell Brasher lives in Trussville, Alabama, where she is working on her first novel. She has published short stories as well as three collections of her *Birmingham Post-Herald* newspaper columns.

Mark Childress, a former staff writer for *Southern Living* magazine, lives in Magnolia Springs, Alabama, where he recently completed his second novel. His first, *A World Made of Fire*, was published in 1984 by Alfred A. Knopf.

Irma R. Cruse lives in Birmingham where she worked for Southern Bell Telephone Company until her retirement in 1976. She holds a Master's degree in English from Samford University and is currently pursuing a second degree in history. She is assistant editor of *The Alabama Baptist Historian* and is currently working on a book about First Ladies.

Virginia Foster Durr, a longtime human rights activist, has been honored by many state and national organizations, including the American Civil Liberties Union, Radcliffe College, and the Southern Women's Archives. She received an honorary doctorate from Wellesley College in 1982. She lives in Montgomery, Alabama.

Jesse Hill Ford published his first novel, *Mountains of Gilead*, in 1961. He has since distinguished himself with a series of novels, short stories, and a play, *The Conversion of Buster Drumwright.* His book, *The Liberation of Lord Byron Jones,* published in 1965, was a full selection of the Book of the Month Club, an international best seller, and a major motion picture released by Columbia in 1969. His most recent book, *The Rider,* was published in 1975. He now lives in Bellevue, Tennessee.

John Forney is Vice Chairman of Luckie & Forney Inc., Advertising in Birmingham. He has been a member of the University of Alabama Football Network Broadcasting team for over 30 years, and is the author of *Crimson Memories, Golden Days.*

Marie F. Gillespie is the author of three books of poetry and is currently working on a novel. She is a member of the Alabama State Poetry Society and a number of other writer's organizations. She lives in Birmingham.

Wayne Greenhaw lives in Montgomery, where he is editor of *Alabama* magazine. He has published six books and written for TV and the movies. He is now working on a novel set in Montgomery in the early 1970s.

Hubert Grissom, Jr. practices law in Birmingham. With his wife, Lucinda, he writes a column for *The Birmingham News.*

Martin Hames lives in Birmingham where he is the Dean of Students at The Altamont School. He has been published by the University of Alabama Press, *The Andover Review, Folio, Chrysalis,* and Kudzu Press.

Ralph Hammond lives in Arab, Alabama. He is president of the Alabama Writers' Conclave and Treasurer of the National Federation of State Poetry Societies. He is the author of twelve books, the most recent of which is *Edging Through the Grass,* chosen as Poetry Book of the Year for 1985 by the Alabama State Poetry Society.

Alvis Howard is a writer who has published a number of articles and stories in a variety of national publications. He lives in Huntsville where he manages a NASA graphic arts, publishing, models and exhibits department for MSI. He has been very active in the revitalizing of downtown Huntsville.

Marie Stokes Jemison is a freelance writer and editor based in Birmingham. Her work has recently appeared in *Southern Exposure, Down Home,* and *Southern Changes.*

Frank Theodore Kanelos is president of The Alabama State Poetry Society, a member of the Alabama Writer's Conclave, and has been listed in the *International Who's Who in Poetry.* He is the author of two published books of poetry and two plays. He lives in Birmingham where he works as director of an outpatient speech-language pathology department.

Helen Shores Lee is the daughter of Arthur Shores, civil rights lawyer and the first black to run for the Alabama state legislature. A former psychiatric social worker, Mrs. Lee is now studying for her law degree at Cumberland Law School. She lives in Birmingham.

Ella Lovelace moved to Alabama in the mid-1800s.

Henrietta MacGuire, a former First Lady of Costa Rica, was married to Jose Marie Hipolito Figueres Ferrer, President of that country from 1952-1958 and 1970-1974. She lives in Montgomery, Alabama, where she is in the real estate business.

Ned McDavid was in the public relations business in New York for many years before retiring to Grayton Beach, Florida. He died in 1985.

Essie Stallworth McGowin moved to Alabama in 1885. She married Greely McGowin, the lumberman who founded the W.T. Smith Lumber Company in Chapman, Alabama.

Smith W. Moseley is a former staff member of the *Birmingham Post, Progressive Farmer,* and *Southern Living.* He retired from *Southern Living* in 1976 and is a columnist and freelance writer. He lives in Birmingham.

Jim Reed lives in Birmingham where he is the proprietor of Reed Books.

Rose Marie Sanders is a partner in the Selma law firm of Chestnut, Sanders, Sanders & Turner. As a municipal judge in Uniontown, Alabama, she was the first black female judge in the state.

Reverend Solomon S. Seay, Sr., a retired minister of the A.M.E. Zion church, was a leader of the black community in Montgomery, Alabama, during the Montgomery Bus Boycott of 1955.

Justice Janie L. Shores was the first woman to be elected to the Supreme Court of Alabama, and is one of the few women in the country now serving on a state supreme court. She lives in Birmingham.

Michael David Shrader, a former police officer, sharpshooter, and advertising consultant, is now semi-retired and living in Birmingham, where he practices gardening, healing, the love of literature, and the fine art of living well.

Ellen Sullivan is the author of two books of poetry and numerous short stories. She lives in Birmingham, Alabama, where she makes her living as a freelance writer and editor.

Sue Walker lives in Mobile, Alabama, where she is editor and publisher of an international journal, *Negative Capability*, and professor of English at the University of South Alabama. She is the author of a book of poems, *Traveling My Shadow*.

Jane L. Weeks headed the Equal Rights Amendment ratification movement in Alabama during the 1970s. She is now Executive Director of the Alabama Indian Commission in Montgomery. She lives in Gardendale, Alabama.

Randall Williams is a writer and editor based in Montgomery, Alabama.

Bettye K. Wray lives in Birmingham where she operates K-Wray Publications. Her published books of poetry are *Early Poems* and *Dear Magnolia*. Her latest collection is titled *Comrades*.